KINGDOM HEROES

TONY EVANS

HARVEST HOUSE PUBLISHERS
EUGENE, OREGON

Cover design by Bryce Williamson

Cover photo © Keith Lance / Gettyimages

Interior design by Rockwell Davis

For bulk, special sales, or ministry purchases, please call 1-800-547-8979. Email: Customerservice@hhpbooks.com

Ⓜ is a federally registered trademark of the Hawkins Children's LLC. Harvest House Publishers, Inc., is the exclusive licensee of the trademark.

Kingdom Heroes
Copyright © 2021 by Tony Evans
Published by Harvest House Publishers
Eugene, Oregon 97408
www.harvesthousepublishers.com

ISBN 978-0-7369-7661-9 (Hardcover)
ISBN 978-0-7369-7662-6 (eBook)
ISBN 978-0-7369-8175-0 (International Edition)

Library of Congress Cataloging-in-Publication Data

Names: Evans, Tony, author.
Title: Kingdom heroes / Tony Evans.
Description: Eugene, Oregon : Harvest House Publishers, [2021] | Includes
    bibliographical references. |
Identifiers: LCCN 2020056269 (print) | LCCN 2020056270 (ebook) | ISBN
    9780736976619 (hardcover) | ISBN 9780736976626 (ebook)
Subjects: LCSH: Bible. Old Testament—Biography. | Heroes in the Bible. |
    Faith—Biblical teaching. | Trust in God—Biblical teaching.
Classification: LCC BS579.H4 E93 2021 (print) | LCC BS579.H4 (ebook) |
    DDC 221.9/22—dc23
LC record available at https://lccn.loc.gov/2020056269
LC ebook record available at https://lccn.loc.gov/2020056270

Printed in the United States of America

21 22 23 24 25 26 27 28 29 / LB / 10 9 8 7 6 5 4 3 2 1

Acknowledgments

I want to thank my friends at Harvest House Publishers for their long-standing partnership in bringing my thoughts, study, and words to print. I particularly want to thank Bob Hawkins for his friendship over the years, as well as his pursuit of excellence in leading his company. I also want to publicly thank Kim Moore and Jean Bloom for their help in the editorial process. In addition, my appreciation goes out to Heather Hair for her skills and insights in collaboration on this manuscript.

CONTENTS

1

WELCOME
TO THE
HALL OF HEROES

The overriding feeling that life isn't working and it's not even worth trying anymore has begun to pervade society at large, causing many people to live with a profound sense of hopelessness and despair. Furthermore, this sense has led more and more of them to throw in the towel on life itself. When nearly 40 million people lost their jobs during the onset of the pandemic-based lockdown in America, suicide rates rose. In fact, during the early months of physical distancing, more people died from suicide in the state of Tennessee than died from COVID-19.[*] Add to that, the overwhelming social, economic, political, and racial unrest we experienced in our culture caused both confusion and insecurity to arise in the hearts of people nationwide.

My phone nearly rang off the hook during the initial stages of these multiple pandemics due to my congregants seeking counsel from me as their pastor. They just couldn't take it anymore. It seemed like each day brought a new worry, fear, or concern to all of us, and my emotions rode the same ever-changing roller coaster of uncertainty everyone else's did.

On top of that, I was at the beginning season of mourning the loss of my wife, ministry partner, and best friend of 49 years, Lois, and I was additionally mourning the loss of my dad, who had passed away just a

---

[*] "Lockdown-inspired suicides on course to DWARF coronavirus deaths in Australia & in time, even in US—studies," RT, May 7, 2020, https://www.rt.com/news/488070-australia-us-coronavirus-suicide-spike/.

month before she did. The previous months had also brought the loss of my sister, her husband, my brother, and two nieces. People were calling me to help them through their pain while I was treading my own painful waters.

So much had suddenly changed in my life. Social situations were different not only because of the loss of so many family members but because of the loss of friends and church members who had passed away. My career routine changed through the temporary closing of our church premises due to the mandatory Dallas County shelter-in-place rules—I stopped preaching to congregations and began preaching to two cameras. Interviews increased as network after network contacted our ministry asking for my perspective on the virus and its social impact, race relations in America, the 2020 election, and more. I stopped traveling to speak at churches, conferences, and events due to being in the high-risk category for COVID-19 based on my age and having had a bout with walking pneumonia at the onset of the pandemic.

Nothing resembled the normalcy I'd once known, lived, and experienced for so long. Nothing at all.

Except God.

In the midst of the chaos of constant change, pounding like waves crashing against breakers set to hold their wrath at bay, God's constancy was calming. And better yet, it remained calming. His power prompted my internal praise. His peace soothed my heart so I could speak comforting truths to the many who looked to me during this strange season we were all sharing as a nation and around the world.

Living by Faith

As each week and month progressed into what seemed like a continual cycle of uncertainty, one day I spoke with my good friend and fellow pastor Jim Cymbala. He'd been away from his church in New York City during the height of the pandemic there, and as was true for so many of those in ministry, his heart was heavy. When he told me a large percentage of pastors in California and New York were considering leaving the ministry due to the difficulties they were facing (at one point, California had even made it against the law to sing in church), the gravity of the reality we were in hit me hard.

Knowing so many were contemplating quitting in the midst of this trial reminded me of those mentioned in Hebrews who had also considered throwing in the towel, hanging up the gloves, and moving on. I'm sure abandoning the faith and going back to the world's ways crossed their minds in hopes that it would lessen the difficulties they faced. Perhaps they even wondered if the Christian faith was worth the effort, because it just didn't seem to be working for them anymore.

In Hebrews 11—often called the Hall of Faith—we're introduced to these individuals and how they responded when life got hard. That chapter is also the basis of our study on kingdom heroes, which is why I'm calling the place we're about to enter the Hall of Heroes Museum. These verses give us both the backdrop and conclusions to the stories we'll explore as we examine the core DNA and features that show up in each hero.

But first, in chapter 10, the author of Hebrews has something important to say to those who want to be kingdom heroes:

> Do not throw away your confidence, which has a great reward. For you have need of endurance, so that when you have done the will of God, you may receive what was promised.
>
> For yet in a very little while,
>
> He who is coming will come, and will not delay.
>
> But My righteous one shall live by faith;
>
> And if he shrinks back, My soul has no pleasure in him.
>
> But we are not of those who shrink back to destruction, but of those who have faith to the preserving of the soul (verses 35-39).

He's telling us what we most need to live as a kingdom hero—endurance. We need the will to keep going when life gets tough. But he also throws in the caveat that we're to have this endurance *based on our faith*. In fact, the way "my righteous one shall live by faith" is worded is important because of what it implies. In other words, faith ought to be our modus operandi. It should be the way we flow. Faith isn't a concept to visit but rather a lifestyle to embrace. Thus, if we're not living by faith, the conclusion based on this passage is this: We're not living righteously. Scripture clearly states that the righteous live by faith.

Are You Living by Faith?

Before we approach the museum, ask yourself this foundational question:

Am I living by faith?

Start here. Start with you. Because if living by faith isn't how you roll, studying the lives of kingdom heroes is useless. You might as well put down this book before we go any further. Sure, you'll gain knowledge from these pages, but without the wisdom and courage to apply it, that knowledge will do you no good. Living by faith is to be a lifestyle for the believer (Romans 1:17).

I encourage you to make the pursuit of increasing the level of faith you put into action your highest priority, not just settling for learning about other people who lived their faith well. God has a destiny for you that can be reached only if you choose to follow Him in like manner. And so, if you've answered yes to the question *Am I living by faith?* I invite you to go through the Hall of Heroes Museum with me. This magnificent place will help you get to know each hero in Hebrews 11 all the more.

Before we go inside the museum, we see an enormous fountain with statues of various kingdom heroes in the midst of it. Let's take a moment to walk around the entire structure and read the statement engraved on it, ensuring we know what a kingdom hero is:

*A kingdom hero is a committed Christian who perseveres by faith
in order to experience spiritual victory and divine approval.*

Now let's step inside, where we see the well-known Hebrews 11:1 displayed in an atrium just outside the hall's entrance. The words are inscribed in large metal lettering, each letter nearly three feet in height, and it spans the width of the area.

*Now faith is the assurance of things hoped for,
the conviction of things not seen.*

You may have memorized this verse at some point, but I don't want you to skip over it just because you feel like you already know it. It teaches us how to live a righteous and victorious life. It instructs us how to go about becoming kingdom heroes ourselves. It lets us know that in order for faith to be faith as God defines it, it must have substance.

Faith isn't an amorphous concept or feeling you find in a faraway land. Nor is it merely an inclination. Kingdom faith means being absolutely sure of the things for which you hope. It involves living with the conviction of things you've not yet seen, a conviction that assures you they will come to pass. This conviction gives you the motivation and strength to endure when life becomes difficult. It gives you the hope to hang on to when sacrifices come into play with the pressures of a pagan or worldly culture.

Faith in Substance

Faith deals with things that are real but haven't yet penetrated our five senses. Faith means actively functioning in the spiritual realm while simultaneously living in the physical realm.

Now, keep in mind that faith is only as meaningful as the substance to which it is attached. Faith has to do with both an expectation and a hope because hope is an expectation about the future. If you have faith in a bad or unreliable substance, that faith won't produce anything. It's like a kid placing faith in the nonexistent tooth fairy. On her own, the tooth fairy won't do anything for that child because she isn't real. But because parents realize their children are placing faith in an unreal entity, they oftentimes leave a surprise under their children's pillows in place of a baby tooth that fell out.

You can apply the same principle to Santa Claus. Santa, on his own, won't bring a single present to anyone, simply because he doesn't exist. But parents see the faith of their children and respond in a way that reinforces that faith—they make surprise gifts appear under the Christmas tree.

Adults place faith in unreal concepts as well. It's just that, by and large, no one follows through on their misplaced faith, and many of them discover that life can come with significant disappointments. After choosing to place their faith in unreal concepts, they eventually learn that the way things turn out doesn't always resemble expectations.

A significant amount of faith placed in an insufficient substance will inevitably produce no results. That's because what makes faith demonstrable is the substance to which it is attached. Thus, if you want to grow your faith, you don't need to go faith-hunting. Rather, you need to focus on a better substance in which to place your faith. Make sure the substance is solid and real. Make sure your faith is in God and in Him alone.

I'll never forget a trip I was scheduled to take to Iowa. My wife, Lois, often traveled with me on my speaking trips, but she didn't want to go on this one because we'd be flying in a small, twin-engine plane.

"You don't have much faith," I said, joking with her.

"That's because you don't have much plane," she responded.

Not until the schedule changed and our new flight would be on a jumbo jet did she change her mind and come along.

"Your faith grew," I told her, laughing as we boarded the much-larger plane.

"That's because your plane grew," she said, smiling in response.

It's a humorous illustration, but the point applies to us all. The size of my wife's faith was directly tied to the size of the plane. That's because, as I've said, faith is related to the substance to which it is attached. True faith in God is tied to a substance that is not yet seen or experienced with our five senses, which is why we must be convinced it's real based on the integrity of God Himself, the One who's calling us to have faith.

Let me put this principle in everyday language: To not live by faith is to call God a liar. Every time you make a decision out of fear rather than by faith in what God has declared, you let it be known that you don't trust that He's telling the truth. I realize none of us would outright call God a liar, but a majority of us do it through our actions or inactions resulting from a lack of faith.

Faith in Action

Now, before we look closely at the lives who modeled faith as told in Hebrews 11, I want to give you a simple definition of faith:

Faith is acting like God is telling the truth.
It's basing your actions on the belief that what He says is true.

Faith isn't merely *feeling* like God is telling the truth. Nor is it *saying* God is telling the truth. For faith to truly be faith, it involves *acting* like God is telling the truth. That's why the Bible calls it walking by faith, not talking by faith or even feeling by faith. This faith walk is to be done without the requirement of prior visible, empirical evidence to validate it (2 Corinthians 5:7). It is rather to be based on the integrity of God.

Faith always includes movement and actions aligned with what you believe to be true. Unless your faith makes it all the way down to your feet, it's not faith. Rather, it's an intellectual concept that hasn't been mixed with action, and nothing concrete will show up in your life. If you want a concrete manifestation of God, then what you believe about Him must be married to what you do in light of that belief. Exercising faith takes God's involvement in your life from a theory in your mind to a reality in your life.

A number of years ago, the church where I serve looked for ways to curb its electricity bills. As a result, we installed motion-detector lighting in certain rooms. That means the lights come on only when motion is detected.

If there's no motion, there's no light. This also means the lights go off on their own when people leave without turning them off. Then the lights come back on when motion is again detected.

Similarly, God will give you the power and light you need when you need it, but He'll wait until He detects motion on your part. If there's no movement in faith, there's no power in your life. The two are tied together. You must trigger the use of His power in your life, and you do that through actions carried out in faith.

God is real. He has great power. But He will not manifest that power in the ways you need Him to until He sees the motion of your life in faith. If there is no movement, His power lies dormant even though it's there to be accessed at any time. It's in living a life of faith that we gain God's approval (Hebrews 11:2).

Here's another way I define faith:

Faith is acting like it's so even when it's not so,
in order that it might be so simply because God said so.

It is in living a life of faith, just like the kingdom heroes the author examines throughout this chapter, that we gain God's approval (Hebrews 11:2).

Why We Need Kingdom Heroes

The Pro Football Hall of Fame is in Canton, Ohio. This is where the football greats—those who exceeded and excelled at the game—are remembered. As you walk the halls of this great museum, you're reminded of what each player did to secure that position. To be enshrined there is no small feat. Only a handful of players, coaches, and owners will ever make it in. Induction requires a rigorous examination of each person as the judges look not only at what they did *in* the game but *for* the game.

God set up His own Hall of Fame in Hebrews 11, where heroes of the faith are recognized for how they modeled what it means to be men and women of heroic faith. And just as the Pro Football Hall of Fame serves as a motivator and inspiration for aspiring football players throughout our land, this Hall of Heroes ought to provide each of us with greater motivation and inspiration for excelling in the area of faith.

When the world of boxing has its championship fights, they bring in the champions of old and introduce them to the crowd before the battle even begins. The throng explodes with enthusiasm as each champion is announced, but the reason they bring them back is to remind those about to battle what's truly at stake—the championship itself.

They also remind the two about to fight it out that others have been in that ring before them. Others have been punched. Others have been knocked down and bruised and bloodied. Yet even though all of that happened to them, they made it through to testify about their victory. Their presence inspires the current fighters to endure the hits, push through the exhaustion, and summon the strength they need to win.

Those we're about to witness in the Hall of Heroes are there to inspire us to keep going. Their lives should motivate us to hang in there, never give up, and stand strong for what we believe in.

Some of you may already feel beaten and bruised. The circumstances of life might have knocked you down, or sin itself may have entangled you. But the Hall of Heroes invites you in to discover that, no matter what you may be facing right now, you can overcome it. If you will simply rise up and place your faith in God through actions aligned under His overarching kingdom rule, you'll experience the freedom and victory you long for.

It's Never Too Late

Now, before we step through the door to the hall, I want to warn you about what you'll see. Some strange people are in there. You and I probably wouldn't have included them all if we were the curators of this place. A liar, a prostitute, a passive man…It's even got people who laughed in the face of God. Some very messed-up individuals are in the Hall of Heroes, I'll admit.

But that should make you smile, because it's good news for all of us. Any of you walking into this hall with me should know that, even if you've made mistakes or fallen far from grace, you can choose to live differently, and you can choose to do it right now. God doesn't set a time limit on faith. You can obey Him now. It's never too late to honor God through a life-style of faith. It's never too late to live as a kingdom hero yourself (and I'll remind you of that again at the end of this book).

To live as a kingdom hero and be qualified for enshrinement in this hall is acting in alignment in faith under God. It means making choices in the physical realm based on what we cannot see but know to be true in the spiritual realm. The author of Hebrews reminds us of this in Hebrews 11:3: "By faith we understand that the worlds were prepared by the word of God, so that what is seen was not made out of things which are visible." Even the word *faith* itself came about through the activity of faith. God spoke into the invisible, and as a result, He created the visible. What we see now was made out of what we cannot see. The entire universe was cre-ated by One we cannot see while using things we cannot see in order to bring about what we can see.

Read the verse in the atrium one more time before we go into the hall itself.

> *Now faith is the assurance of things hoped for,*
> *the conviction of things not seen.*

Faith is all about what we cannot see. It's the conviction of things we cannot see. It involves placing our belief in the spiritual realm to a larger degree than in what we see and experience in the physical realm, trusting that what God says about it is true.

To live by faith is to live with spiritual sight, in tune with a God who can create a universe out of nothing at all. It's a change of perspective from what is right in front of our faces to the truth resident in our spirits through the power of God's Word and the testimony of His Spirit in us. We dem-onstrate our faith in the meteorologist's prediction for rain by picking up our umbrellas as we leave home, even though meteorologists are some-times wrong. But we demonstrate our faith in God, who is never wrong, when we do what He says even when circumstances seem to contradict what He's said.

Rise Up!

As we look around and see a country and world in continual decline, it really is more and more apparent that what we need most is kingdom heroes of the faith. We need men and women who choose to place Christ over culture and conviction over comfort.

And so as we journey through this Hall of Heroes, I pray we will all be inspired by the lives we study to such a degree that we'll become kingdom heroes too. There's no more time for complacent Christianity or ritualistic religion. If we're to impact others for good and advance God's kingdom agenda on earth, we must rise up as the heroes of the faith our world so desperately needs.

2

ABEL,
A MAN
OF WORSHIP

When our kids were young, Lois and I took them to a family camp in New York during the winter. That whole week I served as the guest speaker to the camp attendees, and our family enjoyed a peaceful time. The camp sits on a large lake with the adult facilities on one side of the water and the children and youth buildings on the other, and over the years we created many meaningful memories at this secluded, beautiful, and serene location.

One of the first times we went there, the lake was frozen and the freezing temperatures kept nearly all camp activities inside where it was warm. But when it came time for me to speak to the youth, instead of suggesting we circle the lake to our destination, the person hosting me said we could just walk across it.

"It's shorter this way," he said.

I said nothing in return. I simply looked out at the lake as a whole host of potentially horrific events played out in my mind in fast-forward. As you might imagine, I wasn't too excited about trying to walk across any lake, even a frozen one. I could see myself reaching somewhere in the middle only to hear the ominously haunting sound of ice cracking beneath my feet. That thought alone was enough to keep them firmly planted right where they were—on pavement.

My host noticed my hesitation, and he pointed in the direction of a truck about to cross the lake. Not until I saw it being driven across the ice did I change my mind. My faith suddenly grew stronger as I quickly realized that if a vehicle that heavy could safely cross the frozen lake, surely I could walk across it.

So, after a long pause and a deep breath, I set out, making the phrase *walk by faith* much more personal to me than ever before.

Witnessing something bigger and heavier than me achieve a feat I'd been hesitant to pursue increased my belief that I could do the same. This principle doesn't just apply to frozen lakes, though. It also applies to cold feet when it comes to following God in ways that demonstrate and call for active faith.

As I mentioned in the first chapter, we're studying core tenets of living a life of faith that, when adopted, will give you what you need to live as a kingdom hero. The first one rests as the foundational principle for all else. When you truly understand this aspect of life and what it means to live in light of it, you'll have set the stage for personal spiritual greatness.

Now, you might be surprised by what this tenet is. After all, we rarely attribute much to it other than some entertainment value for ourselves. But that's because we've largely misdefined what it means and how we're to apply it in our lives. The first tenet is worship.

As we begin our journey through the Hall of Heroes, we pass the entry point and round the corner to see our first display—a wall mural of two brothers named Cain and Abel. Abel is shepherding a flock of sheep, and he's staring out at the vast numbers of animals under his care. Cain is tilling the ground with a bountiful harvest. Above Abel are the words *True Worship*.

Now, keep in mind that, when I use the word *worship*, I'm not referring to who your favorite Christian musicians are or how you may like to take walks in nature to lift your spirit. Neither am I talking about how many times you attend church each year, what inspirational verses you post online, or how loud you can say "Amen" and "Hallelujah" while your pastor preaches. Rather, I'm referring to how you choose to honor God through the choices you make with your life.

I realize that isn't what most people think of when they hear the word *worship*, but I'm basing this definition on God's definition, not on what other people think. In fact, Romans 12:1 gives us the most straightforward definition of worship there is.

> Therefore I urge you, brethren, by the mercies of God, to present your bodies a living and holy sacrifice, acceptable to God, which is your spiritual service of worship.

This verse takes the concept of worship to a broader level. Worship isn't just about showing up and singing a few stanzas of a song. Neither is it just about having devotions in the morning, although that is good. To truly worship God requires an overarching frame of mind that governs how you choose to invest the time, talents, and treasures He's given you to utilize for His glory. More formally, worship can be defined as the visible and verbal recognition of God for who He is, for what He has done, and for what we're trusting Him to do.

Worship is so vital to living out a victorious Christian life that it comes as no surprise that the Hall of Heroes in Hebrews 11 starts out with someone who modeled the right way for us to worship—a shepherd named Abel.

Now, you may know Abel best as the man who was killed by his brother, Cain. But when you dig deeper into his story, the reason Abel was killed might surprise you. He wasn't killed over an argument. He wasn't even killed over something he did to deliberately offend Cain. Rather, Abel was killed because he worshipped God in a way that pleased God. He was killed for his true worship.

Before that gets too confusing, let's look at the situation described for us in Hebrews 11:4. In the Hall of Heroes, it's been inscribed on a standing plaque just in front of the wall mural of Cain and Abel. We read,

> By faith Abel offered to God a better sacrifice than Cain, through which he obtained the testimony that he was righteous, God testifying about his gifts, and through faith, though he is dead, he still speaks.

The context of the story of Cain and Abel is found in Genesis chapter 4. There we discover that Abel is the first human of faith because, unlike his parents, Adam and Eve, he didn't get to live in a perfect environment. He didn't have the opportunity of seeing and knowing God face-to-face like his mother and father did prior to sin entering the world. When Adam and Eve sinned, they were removed from the garden of Eden and consequently removed from a direct presence of God.

Following their removal, Scripture tells us, Eve gave birth to two sons. Her first son was Cain, and her second son was Abel. As it says in Genesis 4:2, "Abel was a keeper of flocks, but Cain was a tiller of the ground."

These two young men were both raised in a God-fearing home, not by parents who doubted God's existence. Adam and Eve knew God was real. In fact, God Himself had officiated at their wedding. They were created by Him, literally—"born" not as children but as adults. They'd even experienced walking with God "in the cool of the day" (Genesis 3:8). No, Cain and Abel were not reared in an atheistic environment. They were brought up in a theistic, or God-oriented, home. As a result, they learned about the importance of worshipping God and honoring Him.

Pleasing God with Our Worship

But learning about the importance of doing something and actually doing it are two different things. The next three verses in Genesis 4 reveal this:

> So it came about in the course of time that Cain brought an offering to the LORD of the fruit of the ground. Abel, on his part also brought of the firstlings of his flock and of their fat portions. And the LORD had regard for Abel and for his offering; but for Cain and for his offering He had no regard (verses 3-5).

Both men brought God an offering, yet only one of them pleased Him. One brother did something right while the other brother did something wrong. One did it the way God wanted it done, and the other did not.

Let's look at both the similarities between what the two men did as well as the differences and how they apply to us.

We Can't Please God by Just Showing Up

First, both brothers showed up to worship God. But simply showing up isn't enough. Just showing up doesn't mean God has accepted your worship. Cain showed up, and his worship was flat-out rejected. So as we can see in this passage, two types of people can show up to worship God, even in our contemporary Christian settings. For instance, one person shows up at church with an offering and another one just shows up. But, again, merely bringing yourself to the worship service doesn't cut it. Thus, it's possible to go to worship yet have your worship rejected. It's possible to attend church and have God say, *You've just wasted both your time and Mine.*

I know that sounds harsh, but I want to break down the principles of the passage so you can understand how critical this tenet of kingdom hero living actually is.

We Can't Please God Without Addressing Sin

Second, both Cain and Abel brought an offering for God, and as we'll see later in the passage, they both had a strong desire for Him to accept their offering. Yet only one of them pleased Him. Only one of them had his offering accepted. As verse 5 states, "For Cain and for his offering [God] had no regard." Those are the Bible's words, not mine. God had no regard for Cain's worship.

Why did God show no regard for Cain's offering? We gain insight into that when we examine what worship was designed and established to accomplish—to lead us into the presence of God Himself. Through the posture of worship, we gain access to God's throne and nearness to His heart. Keep in mind, God is holy, and we are not. A person doesn't just walk up to and into His presence on their own accord.

God had already made it clear to Cain and Abel's parents that, to come into His presence, one must address and deal with sin. Adam and Eve tried to cover up their sin by sewing fig leaves together and hiding. But God showed them that wasn't enough. He rejected their fig leaves and instead demonstrated how to address their sin, in that dispensation, by slaying an animal as a sacrifice in order to clothe them in the animal's skins.

In short, neither Cain nor Abel was unaware of what was required as an offering before God. Yet Cain chose to test his limits. He chose to come up with his own set of rules. Rather than find a way to acquire a slain animal, he took the easy path as a tiller of the ground by trade. He gathered some tomatoes, cabbage, and whatever fruit he had and brought it to God. Placing it on the altar, he basically declared, "Here it is, God. I've come to church!" On the other hand, Abel "brought the firstlings of his flock and of their fat portions." He brought a *sacrifice*.

As a result, God had regard for Abel's offering, meaning He consumed it. But toward Cain's offering, He showed no interest at all. To put it in everyday language, God may have said something like, "I'm not doing anything with that, Cain. It's unacceptable." Cain's offering wasn't based on a faith made manifest in his feet—by what he chose to do. He did not fulfill what God had commanded nor at the level God expected or even demanded.

To come into God's presence requires the addressing of sin. It requires an addressing of personal rebellion. It requires addressing whatever it is in a person's life that keeps them estranged from God's presence. To show up without addressing sin didn't cut it for Cain. His refusal to recognize he needed to do things God's way got his worship rejected.

Center Your Worship on Jesus

Now, granted, this was the Old Testament dispensation. This was the season when animal sacrifices provided an entry point to the addressing of sin. But in the church age you and I live in, we no longer sacrifice animals to cover us. Rather, the whole reason Jesus Christ died on the cross was to address our sin and need for atonement. Thus, in our contemporary setting, when people seek to worship God apart from the acknowledgment or awareness of the atonement of Jesus Christ, their worship is not regarded.

That's why our worship must always center on Jesus Christ. He is the sin-bearer in our stead. Far too often today, people go to church like they're going to a club or community center. Rarely if at all do they show any recognition of sin and its impact on their lives, and there's virtually no recognition of the need for forgiveness.

But when people come to church with that mindset, without a heart centered on the atonement of Christ for the forgiveness of their sins, God has not obligated Himself to receive their prayers or worship. Those who come that way might as well have stayed home, because if they're not coming to church on God's terms, He won't accept their worship.

Church is not a club; it's an engagement with God made possible through Christ.

Give God Your Best

Not only did Cain and Abel bring God different offerings, one according to His prescribed way and the other not according to it, but their offerings differed in another way. As we saw earlier, Abel brought the "firstlings" of his flock. He brought the best as well as their fat. He didn't give God junk and leftovers. Rather, he brought the juiciest and most prime he had to offer. But Cain just brought "an offering." He gathered up some veggies and fruit and called it a day.

This leads us to another reason God sometimes rejects much of what we call worship in our lives—we bring Him our leftovers. We simply throw something together and say, "Hey, at least I'm here." We show up to church late. We give God a few minutes before we rush out the door before work, if that. We nod a prayer before a meal or before we go to sleep. Yet leftover worship isn't worship at all. It can be compared to talking with a friend while that friend is consumed by their phone. The whole time you're talking, they're scrolling. Then when you ask a question, all you hear back is, "What? Can you repeat that?"

Unfortunately, that's what most of us do to God all the while expecting Him to give us His best, His favor, His blessing, His covering, His protection, His provision, and more. But as Cain found out the hard way, spiritual connection isn't based on leftovers.

As an example, let's say you went to a restaurant with a friend or family member. A waiter brought out the menu and told you they were serving whatever they couldn't sell from the previous week. You could order any of those leftovers, and they could even mix some together in a soup. Would you order leftovers? Or would you walk out?

I know what I would do. I'd walk out and find a restaurant that knew how to cook fresh food—catch-of-the-day fresh at that. You don't go to a restaurant looking for last week's leftovers. No, you deserve better than that. In fact, leftover-type service often means no tip. Am I right? If a waiter or waitress drops your plate of food in front of you only when they eventually "have the time," you'll probably not leave a tip—if you stay to eat at all.

Or think about this: What if your favorite celebrity, politician, or even your preferred preacher (who might go by the name Tony) is coming to your house for dinner? Would you scramble up some leftovers? I doubt it. You'd want your guest to feel welcomed by what you served.

When some time ago a former president of the United States called my office and said he wanted to visit us on the following Tuesday, you can bet I didn't run out to a fast-food restaurant or gather some leftovers from the fridge. Rather, I set an elaborate lunch in motion so that when he arrived, it would all be ready, hot, and flavorful. I imagine you would do the same.

God sees the level of attention and intention we give to those on whom we want to make an impression and contrasts that with the level of attention and intention we give to Him. And when He sees the difference, He says, *Stop it. Just stay home.*

It's better that you don't even come and waste His time. Again, not my words. This is from the Bible. In Malachi 1:7-10, God puts it this way:

> "You are presenting defiled food upon My altar. But you say, 'How have we defiled You?' In that you say, 'The table of the LORD is to be despised.' But when you present the blind for sacrifice, is it not evil? And when you present the lame and sick, is it not evil? Why not offer it to your governor? Would he be pleased with you? Or would he receive you kindly?" says the LORD of hosts. "But now will you not entreat God's favor, that He may be gracious to us?

> With such an offering on your part, will He receive any of you kindly?" says the LORD of hosts. "Oh that there were one among you who would shut the gates, that you might not uselessly kindle fire on My altar! I am not pleased with you," says the LORD of hosts, "nor will I accept an offering from you."

Take what you give Him to your governor, God says. See if he will accept it. It's a rhetorical question because everyone knows the governor would not accept it. And yet we often do just that to God. We take Him our leftover time, leftover thoughts, leftover energy, leftover investments, leftover praise, and leftover attention while somehow thinking any bone we toss Him should be enough. The audacity most believers have in how they worship God is nothing short of appalling. For instance, some arrive at work on time but don't care what time they get to church. Trust me, I see some of my own congregation trickle in all the way up to the benediction.

"Shut the gates," God says. Stop wasting His time.

Believe God and His Word

Too many are satisfied with giving God not just leftovers but junk food. They have time for everything but God. Bible study curriculum grows shorter and shorter as analytics tell us people just aren't engaging in study as long. Sermons are also getting shorter and shorter, as if they weren't already short enough. Yet most people have no problem giving their favorite sports, teams, and players hours and even days of their time, viewing them in person or on television or listening to sports podcasts.

What Cain suffered from, and what so many of us suffer from today, is the façade of religion. It's like when you take the back-lot tour at Universal Studios and see the façade of buildings where films are made. They're just makeshift little towns showing only fronts. If you were to peek behind them, you'd see nothing there.

We live in this façade of religion, and yet we also want to live as kingdom heroes. We want to walk into miracles, change the world for good, and see the favor of heaven rain down on us. But no hero ever became one by putting on a façade. Heroes are heroes because of what heroes do. They don't just dress up and stand in Times Square for a photo opportunity in exchange for some cash. Real heroes invest the time, effort, and attention necessary to pull off what only heroes can.

Worship God the way He's prescribed us to worship Him—with all of your heart, all of your soul, and all of your mind. Worship cannot be half-stepped or phoned in. It must be done in faith. Yet that level of commitment reveals one reason many of us don't worship by faith—we believe in God without believing God. We mentally believe He exists, but we don't take Him seriously. We don't take His Word seriously. Yet believing God and His Word results in actions and choices that reflect His will and His ways. People who truly believe God is telling the truth in all that He's stated in His Word act like He's telling the truth even if they don't like the truth He's telling.

Here's one more definition I often give for faith:

Faith is simply acting like God is telling the truth.

That means your choices and decisions reflect a heart that believes what He's said is true. If it's true, you'll do it. If what He says about abiding in Him and His Word abiding in you is true, then you'll do it. You'll do it because you're also told that if you do it, you can ask whatever you wish and it will be given to you (John 15:7).

If we truly believe what God said is true, it will show up in our feet. It will be lived out in our actions. But far too many of us hesitate because we, like Cain, want to test the limits. We want to push our way over His way. We want to take what we think is the easy path, all the while setting ourselves on the more difficult path in the long run because we've walked away from God's presence and divine favor.

The Pain of Disobedience

Cain suffered myriad consequences for his lack of commitment, and these consequences led to the disastrous choice of murdering his brother

Abel. But let's not get ahead of ourselves. Cain's consequences didn't start with his crime. A closer look at the passage shows the progression of what happened in his heart and gives us insight into some of the turmoil many believers face today.

We read this next portion as we head past the mural of Cain and Abel in their respective locations, offering their different gifts to God. As we turn the corner, we see a sculpture of the two brothers. Cain is standing over Abel as a boxer would in a fight. Abel is on the ground with blood flowing from the back of his skull. In front of the two, we see a sign that reads,

> Cain became very angry and his countenance fell. Then the LORD said to Cain, "Why are you angry? And why has your countenance fallen? If you do well, will not your countenance be lifted up? And if you do not do well, sin is crouching at the door; and its desire is for you, but you must master it" (Genesis 4:5-7).

Because God had rejected Cain's insufficient worship, Cain became angry, and his countenance fell. He did not immediately choose to murder his brother. A progression of sin within him led him there.

Now, to say that his countenance fell is to let us know that he not only became angry but grew discouraged. He hung his head. His negative emotions took hold. Today we'd say he became depressed and possibly suffered from anxiety as well.

The important principle to realize from this situation is that Cain's lack of authentic worship affected his emotions. His emotional well-being went left because his worship wasn't right. When God became disconnected from his worship, his emotions lost control. As a result, he eventually lost control of his actions as well. The sin crouching at the door became too much for him to bear, and he gave in to its lure toward violence and rage. We see this in the sculpture of the two men before us in the Hall of Heroes—one having killed the other.

A lot of people struggle with emotional instability in our contemporary society. In fact, never has there been a period when so much anxiety, depression, despair, and pain inflected a culture at the level they do now. Large numbers of people are depressed all the time, discouraged all the time, ticked off all the time, frustrated all the time, and can't seem to get along with anyone. They're just off—all the time.

Psychiatrists try to drug us out of depression. Entertainers try to distract us out of sadness. Self-help gurus seek to calm us out of our internal chaos. But until the root cause of all of that is acknowledged and addressed, much of the emotional turmoil plaguing us will remain. There are times when the root cause exists in deep personal loss or difficulty such as grief, as I know all too well. There are also times when the root cause may be found in a chemical imbalance or past traumatic experiences. In these situations, seeking professional help is essential. But there are other times when the root cause is separation from God through an avoidance of dealing with our sin through the grace and mercy of Jesus Christ and presenting our lives as a living sacrifice of worship. It is in those times that no amount of medication or distraction will be effective until the gap between a person and God is addressed.

Cheap worship produces cheap results. If you give God junk, don't be surprised if your emotions reflect junk as well. A great God deserves great honor and worship through your prioritization of His will and His ways in your everyday decisions. Authentic, all-consuming worship ushers in God's favor. A lack of sacrificial worship comes with its own consequences as well.

Zechariah 14:16-19 explains it this way:

> Then it will come about that any who are left of all the nations that went against Jerusalem will go up from year to year to worship the King, the LORD of hosts, and to celebrate the Feast of Booths. And it will be that whichever of the families of the earth does not go up to Jerusalem to worship the King, the LORD of hosts, there will be no rain on them. If the family of Egypt does not go up or enter, then no rain will fall on them; it will be the plague with which the LORD smites the nations who do not go

up to celebrate the Feast of Booths. This will be the punishment of Egypt, and the punishment of all the nations who do not go up to celebrate the Feast of Booths.

Many individuals fail to take God's Word and the precepts He attaches to His covenantal blessings, provision, and favor seriously, so they continue to live in a state of emptiness and emotional turmoil.

Worship is the starting point for your living as a kingdom hero, because without God's presence and access to His power in your life, you'll lack the stability and strength you need to regularly make heroic choices.

Not only did Cain become angry and his countenance fall, but God warned him that sin was crouching at his door, ready to devour him. Cain's emotions had taken over in such a dominate way that sin stood at the ready, seeking to entice him into committing the actions of a villain, not a hero. Cain had become so angry and depressed that it opened a door that had never been opened. That's what happens to many of us when an argument blows up and soon the relationship is over altogether. Or when a little problem and weakness becomes an addiction. Messed-up emotions lead to messed-up actions, which lead to a messed-up life.

When our worship is wrong, our emotions become wrong, and then our spirit soon follows, leading us into the control of sin. Sin can swiftly dominate and control anyone whose spirit is far from God and His presence. This is because if we can no longer control our emotions, we can no longer control our actions. We can't control our words. We can't control our immorality. We can't control our addictions. We can't control our rage. Sin eats us up when emotions become chaotic, just like it ate up Cain's choices all because his worship was off.

Cain got so detached from God that his emotions became a mess, and before he knew it, he'd murdered his brother in spite. Because he was mad at God, he killed someone who had God's favor and pleasure. Jealousy led to first-degree murder (Genesis 4:8). But while Cain may have thought he would get away with it, he was wrong. God called him to account for his actions. We read about this on the next plaque, just beyond the sculpture of the two men, one in a murderous stance.

> The LORD said to Cain, "Where is Abel your brother?" And he said, "I do not know. Am I my brother's keeper?" He said, "What have you done? The voice of your brother's blood is crying to Me from the ground. Now you are cursed from the ground, which has opened its mouth to receive your brother's blood from your hand. When you cultivate the ground, it will no longer yield its strength to you; you will be a vagrant and a wanderer on the earth" (Genesis 4:9-12).

Look under your feet. Do you see that trail of blood on the floor? Don't worry, it's paint and put there for the experience. But it's a reminder that Abel's blood cried out to God for justice. And God delivered. What's more, He put a sign around Cain so no one would be able to kill him and to relieve him of the justice he would otherwise experience (verse 15). God chose to block anyone who sought to remove Cain from his living hell. He wouldn't even let Cain die to escape it.

This is also a reminder to all of us that God judges the sins that destroy the lives of others. Abel's blood spoke to God, giving a verbal testimony (Hebrews 12:24), and based on the testimony of Abel's blood, God rendered judgment and a sentence against Cain (Genesis 4:11-12). In other words, the blood of others has something that renders verdicts from God, so that when people give their lives for spiritual matters or due to persecution while making a difference in history (Revelation 6:9-11), God has the legal right to act on behalf of those faithful believers as they interface with Him in the spiritual realm (Colossians 3:1-2).

No death is in vain when God is involved. He sees all and repays the vengeance due to assailants.

Cain's response spoke loudly of his utter despair due to God's justice: "Cain said to the LORD, 'My punishment is too great to bear!'" (verse 13). Keep in mind, he suffered under the hand of God all because he initially chose to worship poorly. He chose to prioritize his own wants over God's worship. He placed his own desires ahead of God's desires. He did not live out Matthew 6:33, which says, "Seek first His kingdom and His righteousness, and all these things will be added to you."

And just as Abel's blood spoke to God as recorded in Genesis 4:10, we're told in Hebrews 11:4 that Abel still speaks from beyond the grave. His blood rings loud and clear. It carries a message brought on by Cain's consequences. We looked at this verse toward the start of this chapter, but let's read it more closely as we close.

> By faith Abel offered to God a better sacrifice than Cain, through which he obtained the testimony that he was righteous, God testifying about his gifts, and through faith, though he is dead, he still speaks.

The fact that Abel could communicate with God after his physical death about a situation on earth implies knowledge and interaction in the spiritual realm about activities in the physical realm—a concept we will touch on more later.

Abel still speaks, and what he's saying is very important to our lives today. His life and legacy remind us that Cain's choice to place himself above God in the area of worship led to a chain reaction of false religion. And false religion means coming to God like we please, not as He requires.

Cain's example of disobedience and the resulting consequences created such a separation from God that Jude 11 refers to it as a specific way or manner of living: "Woe to them! For they have gone the way of Cain." To go the way of Cain means to give God your leftovers. It involves showing up but not sacrificing. It leads to emotional turmoil, poor choices, and wandering around apart from God's presence. In short, life becomes a living hell. And rather than fulfilling your purpose as a kingdom hero made in the image of the King, you wind up playing the role of villain.

Abel's voice screams from the grave as a reminder to each of us that we must come to God by revelation and not by human reason. God will accept our worship and our entering into His presence only by our doing what He reveals we are to do, not by what we think we should do. It doesn't matter what we think, how we were raised, what the media says, or even what our small groups teach. If it's not God's prescribed way to worship Him—which involves offering our entire selves as a living sacrifice—it's not worship.

Living as a kingdom hero means not relying on our own human reason as the basis for our decisions. Our minds are finite; God is infinite. Living by faith as a kingdom hero means to trust God fully. It means to move on what He says and not on what we feel. It involves thinking based on what He says and not on what we hear. Living as a kingdom hero means aligning our entire life under His overarching kingdom rule.

What About You?

Before we continue our journey, I want you to do a mini self-audit. Ask yourself if you're giving God the time, talents, and treasures He seeks from you. Are you giving Him the first fruits of your energy, thoughts, heart, and soul? Or are you just tossing Him some Froot Loops here or there? You know, the interesting thing about Froot Loops is that, although they come in a bunch of different colors, they all taste the same. No matter what its color, every piece has the same flavor because they're all made from the same stuff.

I don't care what you toss to God or what fancy "color" it is, if it's not what He requires, it all tastes the same to Him. It's unacceptable worship, according to the One who matters most. Yet if you will give Him the worship He requires, your emotions will begin to heal. They will get stronger, more stable. You'll gain access to insights and wisdom you didn't have before. What's more, sin will have to stay behind the door because it won't have any negative energy to piggyback on. As a result, you won't wind up making bad choices, which bring about bad consequences only to leave a lasting legacy of shame.

As we exit this first exhibit in the Hall of Heroes, be reminded that you have a choice. You get to choose whether you'll live as a kingdom hero, a villain, or an extra in this drama called life. It's all up to you.

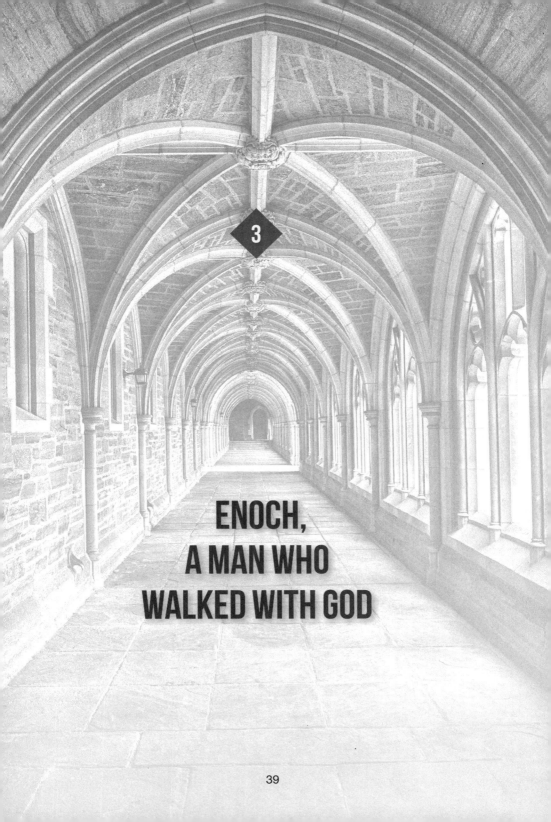

3

ENOCH, A MAN WHO WALKED WITH GOD

Faith is measured by your feet, not by your feelings. It's measured by what you do, not by what you say you're going to do. One of the best ways to determine if you really have as much faith as you think you do is to observe how you respond when things go south. When life goes sideways. When it seems like the world itself has chosen to collapse on top of you all at once, causing you to face a compounding level of issues. That's when you'll be able to judge your authentic level of faith—by the choices you make and the responses you display.

During seasons of high stress, like a boat on stormy seas, you discover what you're truly made of. You learn how strong your faith really is. Anyone can look and talk a good faith game, but not everyone can pull off the faith walk as a kingdom hero should.

So, then, the next tool I want to explore as you gather all you need to live your life as a kingdom hero involves how you walk with God.

As we exit the exhibit on Cain and Abel, we come to another exhibit in the Hall of Heroes, and right above the entryway is the name Enoch. Now, I wouldn't be surprised if you've never heard of him before. Most people haven't. Enoch is a mysterious man to most of us because not much has been written about him in Scripture. But we do know he was a distant descendent of Adam and Eve (Genesis 5:19) and he lived a very long time—365 years (verse 23). And during those 365 years, the Bible also tells us, he strove to be a righteous man, seeking to honor God in all he did. We discover this when we read the first plaque as we enter his exhibit. On it is Genesis 5:21-24:

> When Enoch had lived 65 years, he became the father of Methuselah. After he became the father of Methuselah, Enoch walked faithfully with God 300 years and had other sons and daughters. Altogether, Enoch lived a total of 365 years. Enoch walked faithfully with God; then he was no more, because God took him away (NIV).

One of the important points I want to emphasize from this passage is that Enoch "walked faithfully with God." How you walk with God is an important tool in unleashing your inner hero. If you walk faithfully with Him, you remain close enough to Him to have full access to His wisdom, guidance, and hand on your life. As a result, you will position yourself to experience things unlike most others on earth will. Because Enoch walked faithfully with God, for example, he was given the gift of avoiding one of the major events we dread as humans: death.

Enoch didn't have to die. He never faced that moment when breath slows and then ceases as a person transitions from earth to eternity. Rather, Enoch ascended to heaven alive. That's what we glean from Hebrews 11:5, where we read,

> By faith Enoch was taken from this life, so that he did not experience death: "He could not be found, because God had taken him away." For before he was taken, he was commended as one who pleased God (NIV).

Enoch did not die. Rather, God took him away because He was pleased with him. Talk about a close relationship. God chose for Enoch to skip the part of life so many of us fear. He chose instead to simply draw him even closer through a miraculous and mysterious departure. Enoch's relationship with God models for us what a close, intimate relationship with Him can look like.

Walking in the Spirit

I don't know if you remember this, but a few decades ago, wearing seat belts wasn't required by law. If you do remember, you'll also remember that you could quickly tell how close a couple was relationally by how close to each other they sat in the car. Before seat belts were put in place, causing us all to remain apart and safely strapped in, at times a couple in love would sit so close together that you might not even be able to tell who was driving. It looked like two people were sitting behind the steering wheel.

You could also tell when things weren't right between a couple, because while one was driving, the other was hugging the opposite door. The distance itself served as an indicator for whether they were experiencing relational intimacy.

Enoch and God knew no spiritual distance between them at all. Enoch walked faithfully with God, and in doing so, he pleased Him. Keep in mind, this was Enoch walking with God and not God walking with Enoch. That's an important distinction to make, because most people want God to walk with them. They say, *This is where I'm going, God, and You can join me.* But that's not what God requires of His kingdom heroes. He requires us to walk with Him to where He's going. We're to find out what His agenda involves and what His focus is on and then take part in that, not the other way around.

Enoch walked with God. That means he had to start by tracking where God was going. Then he had to take the necessary faith steps to join Him.

The New Testament phrase for walking with God is to *walk in the Spirit*, found in Galatians 5:16. (Some translations say walk *by* the Spirit, meaning with the Spirit.) When you walk in the Spirit, you're walking according to the Spirit's leading. It means taking step after step according to the Spirit's guidance based on God's Word. It doesn't involve a hop, a skip, and a jump. Walking in the Spirit is not a leap. Rather, it's a walk. That means it's an ongoing, progressive decision you make throughout your time on earth.

Scripture tells us Enoch began to walk with God after he turned 65 years old. We don't know what caused the delay, but we know he eventually got it right. What's more, because he lived so long, he walked faithfully with God for 300 years. That's a very long time to remain consistent. In fact, taking place over an extended period of time, that would be considered a marathon walk, not a sprint.

To walk with God is to bring Him and His viewpoint to bear on the steps you take in life. It means God becomes the primary part of your decision making. He's the driver of your thought processes. He doesn't just get scheduled into your calendar. Instead, He influences the entirety of your calendar. Walking with God means aligning your heart, soul, and mind under His rule as you cultivate an intimate relationship with Him.

Not too long ago, we had an outdoor photoshoot scheduled for some upcoming promotional items for our ministry. Due to my full calendar, it had been scheduled for nearly a year, so it was important to get it done. Unfortunately, it rained on the day of the photoshoot. In fact, it poured during parts of it, a storm complete with the loudest thunder I'd heard in a long time. We had to get creative.

Some awnings were available for me to stand under so I wouldn't get wet, but getting there required walking in the rain. Needless to say, I didn't always manage to stay dry, even with an umbrella. This was because I was walking in a wet environment, with both moisture and raindrops.

To walk in the Spirit, or to walk with God by faith, means to walk in an atmosphere of God's influence and control—an environment where His perspective invades and affects all you do. If God isn't influencing the steps of your movement except on Sundays or a few other times you allot for Him, you're not walking in the Spirit. Rather, you're visiting the Spirit. And visiting the Spirit is not the same as walking in it. Neither will it produce the same results.

To walk in the rain is to experience the effects of the rain. To walk with

God is to experience the effects of God. It means including Him in all aspects of your life. Every decision. Every thought. Every dream. To walk with God is an all-encompassing experience.

Now, if you walk with someone else, either for exercise or pleasure, that person is probably someone you like. I would be surprised if you chose to walk with someone you didn't like. That's because to walk with someone is to spend time with them. It's to do something in harmony with them. It's to match the cadence of your strides with theirs so you remain side by side. If you didn't care for the person or they annoyed you the whole time, your walk together would end up being very uncomfortable. Amos 3:3 puts it this way: "Do two walk together unless they have agreed to do so?" (NIV). In other words, it's hard to walk with those with whom you have conflict.

To walk with God similarly assumes you are in agreement with Him. If you're disagreeing with God about anything at all, it will be hard to walk in step with Him. It will be hard to hang out together simply because you're not on the same page. You're not walking with someone if you're on two different sides of the street.

To stroll with God, then, means you've already decided you want to go where He's going. You welcome His unrestricted presence in your life.

Get Close to God

To walk with God also assumes a shared nature. God is Spirit, and when you accepted Christ as your Savior, you accepted the Holy Spirit into your life. Your spiritual life was born anew so that you now share a spiritual nature with God Himself.

Consider this: You can take your dog for a walk, but you can't walk with your dog because, when it comes to natures, you and your dog don't have anything in common. You can't turn to your dog and say, "Fido, what do you think about this?" and expect to get any reasonable response. Your dog can't respond with much more than a bark, whine, or growl. And while you can take a guess at what each of those means, you will never know for certain. Why? Because you have no shared nature.

With God, because He is Spirit and you are relating to Him spiritually, you're able to exchange information in a way that is understood by both sides. God is not a stranger to your thoughts, hopes, and desires. Rather, you walk with Him daily as a continuous form of mutual exploration and communication. That means harmony and a shared spiritual perspective.

In order to do this, we must walk by faith, believing that God is actually there. I realize that might sound elementary, but I believe that's where most of us get hung up and fail to use this kingdom tool well. See, it's hard to walk with someone if you're unsure they're even there. That's why I believe Hebrews 11:6 states, "Without faith it is impossible to please God, because anyone who comes to him must believe that he exists and that he rewards those who earnestly seek him" (NIV).

If you don't believe you're walking with God, you will not commune with Him. If you doubt He's even there, how can you expect to hear from Him? Far too many believers doubt God's manifest presence in their lives. Because they can't physically see Him, they fear He doesn't truly abide near them. Sure, God may exist somewhere out there in never-never land, a lot of Christians think, but it's hard to believe He exists right there next to them. Close enough to talk to. Near enough to notice. And this reality is reflected in the lack of prayer as a lifestyle.

Too many see God as merely a cosmic force somewhere in the universe. He's big enough and wise enough to hang the stars, but He lacks any real ability to communicate with us or make Himself known in ways we can understand. But God is more than just a force. He is not a concept. Nor is He just a creator. God is a personal Being, and, therefore, He is knowable. He is relatable. He has emotions. The Bible gives us many examples of God's emotions. And what's more, He wants to engage with you and me on a daily basis to show us what to do, how to respond, where to go, and what decisions we can make to live a life that pleases Him and brings us peace and purpose.

God wants a relationship with you. He's not seeking visitation rights on the weekend; He wants full custody. Yet if you choose to view Him only through a religious lens and not a relational lens, you'll miss out on the meaning He can bring to your life. I understand that not seeing God physically hinders many from acknowledging His presence and engaging with Him regularly. But that's why faith undergirds the use of this tool, walking with God. You must have faith that God is there in order to relate to Him personally.

This truth reminds me of a story about a teacher who was an atheist. She asked her kids in the class if they could see the trees outside the window.

One of the kids answered, "Yes, I can see the trees."

Then she asked another question: "Can you see the flowers?"

Another kid answered, "Yes, I can see the flowers."

"What about the sky?" she asked. "Who can see the sky?"

"I can," each kid answered as they raised their hands.

The teacher lowered her voice. "Can you see God?"

One of the kids on the front row answered, "No, I can't see God."

"Then He must not exist," she responded.

To which the kid replied, "But can I ask you a question?" The teacher nodded. "Can you see your brain?"

Laughing, she said, "No, I can't see my brain."

"Then it must not exist," the wise child responded, causing the entire class to erupt in laughter.

You and I believe in many things we don't see. Just because we can't see God doesn't mean He's not there. In fact, we see His impact and creative hand all around us. We see the results of His Being in everything that exists. So not seeing Him physically shouldn't keep us from drawing close to Him in our daily walk. God will respond to our belief when we demonstrate it by committing our time, focus, and intention toward getting to know Him as we regularly walk with Him.

If, then, we're to walk with God, first we need to believe that He exists and that He desires to have a relationship with us. Second, according to Hebrews 11:6, we need to believe He rewards those of us who diligently seek Him. When we believe He is real and pursue an intimate relationship with

Him, He will reward us. God is both personal and responsive. He will not waste our time on a journey of pursuit in walking with Him. We will not regret the moments we spend in His presence, the memories we make by His side, or the miracles He performs both in and through us as we walk closely with Him.

When you and I choose to take God seriously by walking step-by-step with Him, not as an event but as a lifestyle, we experience His power in our lives. He will pull off things most people think are entirely impossible. After all, the way Enoch left earth would be considered impossible. We read earlier that "he could not be found, because God had taken him away." This is because how you live will often determine how you leave.

Nobody dies the exact same way, but Enoch had been walking with God for so long and so closely that God eventually just took him home alive. After 300 years of walking together and Enoch's bringing God's viewpoint to bear on every situation in his life, God said, in a manner of speaking, "Let's just keep on going." They were closer to heaven by that point anyhow, so the two of them just kept walking.

God can provide miracles like this in your life, even to such a degree as Enoch experienced, if you will just make your relationship with Him a priority. The thing you fear the most—whatever it is—doesn't need to alarm you. When the time comes for you to go through it, God will be there. He will hold your hand. He will guide you where you need to go. You may not be able to see the path to take, but God knows it. He can show you the way so that, when all is said and done, you can say like Job, "When He has tried me, I shall come forth like gold" (Job 23:10).

Life isn't always easy. In fact, rarely is it easy. Unleashing your inner hero won't take place simply because you decide to do so. It will take effort, strength, and even pushing through life's pains. But remember, one of the reasons people choose to walk together is to bear the burden of the journey together. Somehow, having someone alongside you makes the hills a little easier to climb. It provides each person with a positive distraction from the pain so they can move forward in peace with perseverance. Thus, when you include, engage, and relate to God on a personal level regarding every aspect of your life, He becomes that walking partner to propel you forward.

Your Personal GPS

Not only does God become your walking partner for encouragement, hope, and strength, but walking with Him gives you the opportunity to follow Him. Who better to follow than the One who knows where you need to go?

Those who know me or have listened to my sermons over the years won't be surprised by this, but when it comes to technology, I have a long way to go. Even so, I've been slowly learning how to live in this new world of gadgets galore. The lockdown of 2020 helped speed that learning curve a lot, simply because all my normally in-person meetings were now being held on this thing called Zoom. I had to learn how to position myself to be seen in a way I wasn't used to. In fact, at one point I even had to learn how to preach from my living room.

On top of that, radio and podcast interview requests kept coming in due to all the issues arising in our nation, and in order to do the interviews, I had to learn how to talk to my iPad. And then, not too long into the pandemic, I got my very first laptop so it could be dedicated for interviews, on a table along with a small light and microphone. As long as no one touched my laptop or changed any of the settings on it, it would be ready each time I needed it.

But I did have a previous growth moment long before the pandemic when I'd offered to drive our pastoral staff to a meeting in downtown Dallas. I got behind the wheel of my car like normal, with the directions printed on paper like normal, only to have everyone else in the car look at me as if I were acting abnormally.

"What are you doing?" one of my associate pastors asked with a look of shock.

"I'm reading the directions."

He looked at my hand with the paper, and then he looked at my other hand on the wheel. He then looked at the screen in the middle of my console, which was dark. "You do know you have a GPS that will tell you where to go, right?" he asked. "You don't need that paper anymore."

I had heard about the GPS thing, so I told him I was aware. But then I went back to looking at the paper in my hand. That's when he decided to take things into his own hands and started pushing a number of buttons on the screen. Once he'd finished, a map pulled up and a voice I'd never heard spoke, telling me where to go.

"Pastor, see, you are the arrow," my associate pastor explained to me, pointing to the screen. "Your arrow will follow this line while you keep listening to the invisible person, and she'll also guide you if you need additional help."

I admit, the GPS and the invisible person did help us get to our location a lot easier than if I'd stuck with using my paper. But in order for them to do so, I had to be willing to learn to use something I wasn't used to using.

You may not be used to hearing the voice of God. You may not be used to walking with Him. And it might be a little challenging to start including Him in everything in your life all day, all week, all year long. You may even forget to ask His perspective when things get hard. But if you'll familiarize yourself with this tool God has given you—walking with Him—and learn how to use it, you'll get where you're going with greater ease and at a faster speed than ever before. He will lead you into the fulfillment of your destiny as you follow His direction.

God has given each one of us who know Him through His Son, Jesus Christ, a personalized navigational system to guide us. This spiritual GPS has a specific name as well: the anointing. The anointing is a supernatural guidance system placed within you to help steer you in the direction God has planned for you. First John tells us, "You have an anointing from the Holy One, and you all know" (1 John 2:20).

Right away we're told that whatever this anointing is, as kingdom followers we have it. Those who are Christians have it. A few verses later John says, "As for you, the anointing which you received from Him abides in you" (verse 27). Saying that it abides in you is just another way of saying it's built into the vehicle. My GPS unit abides in my car whether or not I use it. Similarly, the GPS called the anointing abides in you as a child of the King. It's up to you to activate and use it to your advantage.

If you choose not to listen to your navigation system, you're going to wind up tuning into someone else's GPS. Something or someone will guide you. You get to choose what or who. But you need to choose wisely in order to live as a kingdom hero, because anyone or anything outside of God won't be taking you toward the same destination God has in mind.

What's more, God's specific directions for you may not be the same today as they were yesterday. You have to understand your spiritual GPS, because God may give you different routes for the same problem on different days. While God never changes, His methods often do. That's why it's so critical to stay closely connected with Him as you walk beside Him each step of the way.

First Corinthians 2:12 says we receive the Spirit "so that we may know the things freely given to us by God." The Bible is clear: the Holy Spirit's job is to anoint you and activate you that you might know what God wants of you specifically. The goal of the Holy Spirit is to make God's will, guidance, and intention experiential in your life. His job is to make God's plan real and actualized in your life.

In 2 Kings chapter 6, we read about how a prophet named Elisha was preparing to face an enemy army with a servant who was terrified. No surprises there. Elisha tried to calm his fears and subdue the frantic nature of his heart: "Do not fear, for those who are with us are more than those who are with them" (verse 16). Then Elisha prayed, "Lord…open his eyes that he may see" (verse 17). The Bible says God then removed the scales from the servant's eyes, and the servant saw that "the mountain was full of horses and chariots of fire all around Elisha" (verse 17).

Because Elisha had the anointing, he could see things the servant couldn't. The anointing helps you see with spiritual sight so you know how to react in the circumstances of life. As recorded in the New Testament,

God opened the martyr Stephen's eyes as he was being stoned. Acts 7:55 says, "Being full of the Holy Spirit, [Stephen] gazed intently into heaven and saw the glory of God, and Jesus standing at the right hand of God." This spiritual sight allowed Stephen to pass through the fire of persecution with peace and forgiveness toward his offenders.

Keep in mind, God opened Stephen's eyes because of his closeness to the Spirit. He was walking with the Spirit. Walking with God enables you to walk through the most difficult days a human can face, with both dignity and grace.

Going Against the Grain

Walking with God means you'll experience greater guidance, more penetrating levels of peace, and personal encouragement. Not only that, but walking with God means you'll be walking against the grain of the culture. Enoch marched to a different drumbeat, not being directed or defined by the ungodly values of the day. We know this by the brief summary statement we come across as we walk through the exhibit on Enoch in the Hall of Heroes.

Painted on one wall is an image of an ungodly culture, along with one man standing against it, strong and confident while the culture unravels around him. Then beneath the painting we read these words from Jude 14-15:

> It was also about these men that Enoch, in the seventh generation from Adam, prophesied, saying, "Behold, the Lord came with many thousands of His holy ones, to execute judgment upon all, and to convict all the ungodly of all their ungodly deeds which they have done in an ungodly way, and of all the harsh things which ungodly sinners have spoken against Him."

It's important to note that Jude specifically references which Enoch he's talking about in this passage—the Enoch who was in the seventh generation from Adam. This isn't the same Enoch known as Cain's son, mentioned in Genesis 4:17: "Cain had relations with his wife and she conceived, and gave birth to Enoch; and he built a city, and called the name of the city Enoch, after the name of his son."

The Enoch who was Cain's son was known by mankind because he had a whole city named after him. As far as we know, he did not pursue God or live a life of righteousness. The Enoch in the Hall of Heroes, however, who was the seventh generation from Adam, was not known or recognized by mankind. He left no real legacy. He had no reputation. He didn't even have a burial. But he was known by God. He walked with God. And when the time came for him to depart, he left with God as well.

So the question for you is this: Who do you want to know your name? Do you want to be an earthly hero who's here today and gone tomorrow? Or do you want to be a kingdom hero who draws the attention of angels and is known by God Himself? You get to choose. You can live for other people and fame, or you can live for God and experience the mysterious, powerful miracles of His hand.

Let me remind you of this, though: Worldly fame is passing. People may know you today but not tomorrow.

I learned this firsthand when Lois and I went to Israel with our ministry a few years ago. Three of our kids went on this trip as well, and one of them was my daughter, Priscilla Shirer. Her presence allowed for some team-teaching on specific locations. You've probably heard of Priscilla by now. Most everyone I run into has. Her roles in blockbuster films such as *War Room* and *I Can Only Imagine* have made her a household name in many Christian circles. Not only that, but she's a dynamic speaker as well!

That being said, you probably won't be surprised to hear that while the two of us were filming a portion of our Bible study at the garden of Gethsemane, we were suddenly swarmed by a tour bus group of women wanting a picture with…Priscilla. Yes, I, who'd often been approached by people who recognized me, stood to the side as they all rushed up to my daughter to grab a photo with her. But I just smiled inside, knowing how quickly being well-known can be pushed aside. In certain places, Priscilla used to stand off to the side so people could greet me. Now I was the one there!

People from one "tour bus" may know you, but then the next one pulls up, and those people push you out of the way to get to someone else! Worldly recognition is temporary at best. That's why making it your sole pursuit is foolish.

Kingdom heroes don't compromise with ungodliness to be popular or to have a big name or a big house and a lot of followers on social media. A kingdom hero who walks with God knows not to mix diesel with unleaded, because if they do, they'll wind up going nowhere. The engine of their spirit hasn't been made to mix the fuel that drives them. It must be pure and straight from the Source Himself.

Practice Walking with God

Now, again, you may not be used to walking with God, so I understand this will take a little practice. When children learn to walk, they fall down far more than they take successful steps. And if you start an exercise program, you don't begin by walking ten miles a day. You do what you can and go as far as your body will let you. Your body is simply not used to doing so much. But if you persist and keep walking, you'll build up the stamina to go farther each day.

Let me tell you a secret that helps to build up your walking stamina. The secret is to walk with someone you don't just like but can really talk to. The conversation on those walks will help distract you from the frustration and perspiration of the walk itself. So for your spiritual walk, talk to God. He's right there with you, and He wants to see you develop your spiritual muscles of faith.

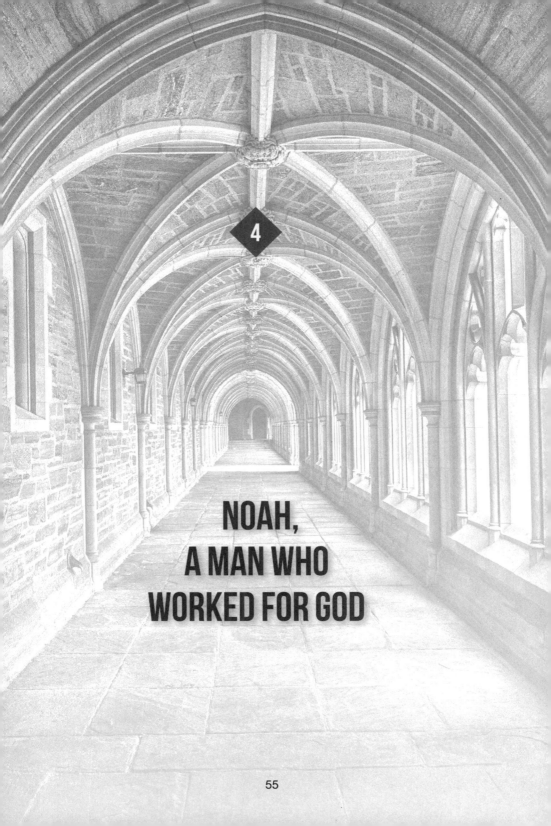

4

NOAH,
A MAN WHO
WORKED FOR GOD

When it comes to hair, you probably know about the fad once known as the Jheri curl. If you don't, then let me tell you about one of the most popular trends to hit our African-American culture.

The Jheri curl was a permanent-wave hairstyle that specialized in transforming coarse hair into a glossy, more loosely curled look. It was also much easier to care for than hair with other chemical treatments, and it soon spread like wildfire. In the 1980s, nearly everyone with coarse hair—male or female—sported the Jheri curl. I did too. That's why I can tell you firsthand that keeping the curls from drying out became a top priority for most of us. Once they dried out, the look lost its luster...and fast.

So to keep our hair from drying out, we would keep some curl activator nearby. Trust me, keeping it close was essential. We didn't want to be caught with dry curls looking flat. In fact, not much looked worse than a dried-out Jheri curl. When the curls began to dry out, we'd spray on the activator, then massage it in a bit and allow it to work its way through to give us back the curl. The activator would connect with our hair where the perm from the Jheri curl had been placed, and it would essentially reignite and moisturize the curl, bringing it back to life. In short, the activator gave us back our curl.

Dried-Up Faith

Many of us fail to live our lives as kingdom heroes simply because our faith has dried up. We go through the motions only to discover that our Christian walk has gone flat. We talk about believing in God, but the power has fizzled. The luster has been lost. The shine has dimmed to a flicker. When the faith we need to fully experience the victory of kingdom living has faded and fallen to the wayside, heroic actions to advance God's kingdom remain dormant within.

So many of us lack the robust expression of faith we were created to have because we're missing faith's activator. We lack that which transforms the heart of faith to the next level of heroic fruition.

James explains this.

> What use is it, my brethren, if someone says he has faith but he has no works? Can that faith save him? If a brother or sister is without clothing and in need of daily food, and one of you says to them, "Go in peace, be warmed and be filled," and yet you do not give them what is necessary for their body, what use is that? Even so faith, if it has no works, is dead, being by itself (James 2:14-17).

James lets us know a faith that produces nothing at all exists. It is not active. It doesn't work. It's dried out. But he also lets us know how to reactivate faith—by combining what we do with what we believe. That brings it to life again. The work of obedience ignites the reality of faith so we see the invisible spiritual power enter into the visible reality around us.

This truth is tied to what we read earlier in Hebrews 11:1: "Faith is the assurance of things hoped for, the conviction of things not seen." Conviction always produces action. Convictions inform and inspire what we do, not just how we feel. Yet because so few Christians today live with much conviction at all, we're no longer seeing God operate through the body of Christ as He once did.

Similarly, believers are limiting God's miraculous intervention in their lives because they're trying to live with a dried-up, shriveled spirit. Yes, they may be saved and on their way to heaven, but they fail to witness heaven joining them on earth simply because God can't get them to work out their faith through actions. For faith to be real, it must be tied to something tangible you do.

Now remember, faith is not founded on what you feel. You can feel no faith at all but still be full of faith if you act in obedience to God based on what He says. Similarly, you can feel like you're full of faith and yet have no faith because you choose not to step out and move forward on what you've been shown to do. Walking by faith always involves movement. Without movement, there is no faith. You can shout, clap, holler, and even flip a pew in faith if you want to, and yet you'll have no *living* faith if you don't obey what God has revealed for you to do. If your feet don't move, your faith is dead.

We're facing an epidemic of indecisiveness in our culture today. So many people are simply afraid to make a decision. And the concept of groupthink has taken on a whole new meaning to such a degree that it's become a choke hold. Far too many of us wait for consensus from everyone and their brother and their cousin before moving ahead on anything. The existence of "cancel culture" has played into this fear of decision making.* As a result, more often than ever, we as believers fail to move forward based on what God has directed us to do.

Just think about what would have happened if Noah had waited for consensus on building the ark. None of us would be here today. He would not have built the ark. When the floods came, the entire population would have been wiped out. Game over.

Thankfully, though, Noah's faith had been activated. He had a living faith that showed up in what he did, not just in what he said. As a result, his legacy is on display in the Hall of Heroes. His impact has gone down in history as one of the bravest, most courageous to have ever been lived out.

---

* From *Merriam-Webster's Collegiate Dictionary*, 11th edition: "*Cancel culture* [has] to do with the removing of support for public figures in response to their objectionable behavior or opinions. This can include boycotts or refusal to promote their work." Of course, the behavior and opinions are objectionable as they are *perceived* to be.

Now we exit the exhibit on Enoch and head down a long hallway with murals of animals grouped in twos on each side. The faint smell of hay and stable animals fills the air, and we hear the different sounds the creatures make. As we near the end of the hallway to enter the next exhibit, a light drizzle comes down from the ceiling. You're startled because you didn't expect to see rain in a place like this. But neither did anyone expect rain in Noah's day. The point has been made.

Once we enter Noah's exhibit, our eyes come upon an enormous replica of a half-built ark, and a man is working diligently to build it. In front of the ark are these words inscribed on a sign:

> By faith Noah, being warned by God about things not yet seen, in reverence prepared an ark for the salvation of his household, by which he condemned the world, and became an heir of the righteousness which is according to faith (Hebrews 11:7).

Noah arguably gives us the greatest illustration of faith at work in humanity. His story highlights a man of incredible conviction. He didn't fear "cancel culture." He didn't strive for popular acceptance. He knew God and chose to follow Him closely.

Looking more closely at his character will help us discern just how he pulled off such a feat of heroic faith. As we walk past the half-built ark and enter the next portion of his exhibit, we see the words from Genesis 6:8-9 inscribed on the wall in front of us. These words about this unique man give us a glimpse into the qualities that made him a true kingdom hero.

> Noah found favor in the eyes of the LORD. These are the records of the generations of Noah. Noah was a righteous man, blameless in his time; Noah walked with God.

After reading the words, we take a moment to look at the image of him painted on the wall next to them. His appearance is like any other man's, but something in his eyes draws us in. It's hard to describe, but if we were to put what we see into words, they might be *stability* or *confidence*. It's not pride; it's peace. And what seems to strike us most is an entire lack of fear.

After all, Noah had little to nothing to fear because he lived to please God. He walked with God, similar to the many others who also wound up in the Hall of Heroes. On top of that, Noah was a blameless man. He had integrity with both people and God. As a result, he found favor with God. And out of all things to hope for or seek during a person's time on earth, favor with God should always be a top priority. God's favor can make a way out of no way. God's favor can reverse what seems to be an irreversible situation. God's favor can do more than bring blessing; it can bring peace.

Since Noah walked in proximity to God, he experienced His favor, which, in his case, spared his life and his family's lives as well.

Most of us know the story of Noah and the ark from our earliest Sunday school lessons. Even non-believers have heard of him and his ark. But what makes Noah's walk of faith and actions of obedience all the more admirable is considering the kind of culture he lived in before the flood. Noah was walking with God in a cultural context when no one else walked with God at all. Talk about peer pressure. Every other inhabitant family on the planet had strayed far from God. Not only that, but humanity had so deeply diverged into demonic activities and sinful lifestyles that God had chosen to wipe out everyone and start again. It was so bad that only a complete reset would do.

Turning away from the image of Noah, we look behind us to see another mural. This one shows debauchery, cultural demise, human sacrifice, sin, and sheer evil. Genesis 6:1-7 is written on a sign in front of the monstrous images and explains what's going on.

> It came about, when men began to multiply on the face of the land, and daughters were born to them, that the sons of God saw that the daughters of men were beautiful; and they took wives for themselves, whomever they chose. Then the LORD said, "My Spirit shall not strive with man forever, because he also is flesh; nevertheless his days shall be one hundred and twenty years." The Nephilim were on the earth in those days, and also afterward, when the sons of God came in to the daughters of men, and they

bore children to them. Those were the mighty men who were of old, men of renown.

Then the LORD saw that the wickedness of man was great on the earth, and that every intent of the thoughts of his heart was only evil continually. The LORD was sorry that He had made man on the earth, and He was grieved in His heart. The LORD said, "I will blot out man whom I have created from the face of the land, from man to animals to creeping things and to birds of the sky; for I am sorry that I have made them."

Did you catch that last line? God was sorry He'd made mankind. The entire world was wicked. Culture was filled to overflowing with immorality, violence, lewdness, vulgarity, profanity, lying, killing, blasphemy, and demon possession. The fallen sons of God had cohabited with the daughters of men. The fallen sons of God are also known as the fallen angels. These fallen angels were demonized men who had relationships with women, which, in turn, gave birth to a demonized hybrid population. Demonic thoughts, patterns, control, oppression, and sheer malevolence had infiltrated humanity to such a degree that people were having to come up with new ways of doing wrong.

As a result, God grieved His decision to create humanity; His heart hurt at what He saw. And when He recognized that every intention and every thought in man's heart and mind was only evil, He decided to intervene to bring a swift end to it all. The Bible doesn't go into great detail on this, but, in fact, it's important to note that it does tell us God had even chosen to blot out animals, from the creeping things to the birds that flew. Everything had been contaminated at some level.

We shouldn't be surprised at the rapid spread of contamination, because filth does just that when given the right atmosphere to thrive. For example, if you were to leave some open bins filled with leftover food scraps in your garage, you'd soon find a swarm of flies and an army of roaches there within just a day or two—maybe even in a few hours. Left long enough for the flies to breed and the roaches to multiply, you would then have maggots, mice, and rats as well. If the mice and rats were given enough time to make your garbage-filled garage their home, you would see snakes too. This is because each new level of filth and its feeders would send an invitation to an even more grotesque guest.

Sin spreads, which is why demons are drawn to sinful people, where they find the opening they need to enter hearts and make themselves at home. If you've studied angels and demons at all, you're aware that demons require a host in which to live out their lustful and destructive desires. Demons are spiritual beings, and to carry out their damaging exploits, they need to connect themselves onto or inside a host. Once someone has opened the door for demons to enter, they quickly set up camp and settle in.

This is how sin turns into addiction, and it's one reason it's so hard for addicts to get over certain sinful habits. By the time the sin is amplified into an addiction, the demons have taken over. Now the person is no longer just dealing with the sinful behavior and chemical reactions the body produces in its response but is also fighting demonic invasion. And far too often they're fighting their addiction with little or no spiritual insight into how to fight it well.

This is why it's so important to keep your heart, mind, and life pure on an ongoing basis. Keep it clean. Just as it's important to regularly take your trash to the curb or dumpster rather than allow it to pile up in your home, it's important to take out the trash of sin from your soul on a regular basis. You do this through awareness, acknowledgment, and regular repentance of sin.

Ignoring sin is about as smart as letting your meal leftovers pile up on the kitchen counter. Can you imagine what that would look like, smell like, and feel like after a week? Apply that visual example to your soul and spirit. Remember what happened to Cain when he didn't address his sin? When we allow sin in our lives to go unaddressed, we create a dirty, infested environment where demons and demonic influence will multiply.

Every homeowner or renter knows to take out the trash on a regular basis. Unfortunately, though, not as many Christians realize the importance of the cleansing power of repentance from sin. Kingdom heroes recognize the need to routinely address sin in their lives. This is a starting point to activating faith's power.

The Pressure of Culture

Kingdom heroes also know not to cave in to the culture. I'm sure Noah faced a lot of pressure to condone and take part in the existing cultural norms around him. Yet he remained consistently righteous and faithful to God. I bring up this point because more and more so these days, we as Christians are living in a highly pressurized society. Voices and influences all around us are trying to get us to buy into the ideology of the contemporary culture and go along with it.

Maybe this sounds familiar to you. Some of you work in a pressurized environment. You're under pressure to do things you shouldn't do or do things in ways you shouldn't do them. Or pressure might be coming from your friends or family members. Even social media puts a lot of pressure on people to conform to certain thoughts, words, and actions. We all face a considerable amount of pressure to submit to societal norms. This pressure can begin to squeeze you so tightly that you feel like you're going to burst. So rather than continue in the uncomfortable feeling, you compromise what you believe in just to fit in. Just to relieve the pressure.

I'm sure you'll agree that it's easy to be a Christian in church. Few if any competing voices exist there because everybody basically agrees with everybody else. And even if they don't agree, some people will pretend they do. But when you go back into the world—into your work, your home, your social circle, or by any other way—that pressure builds. What's more, that pressure can become dangerous.

If you were to go deep enough under the surface of an ocean without addressing what's called hydrostatic pressure, your body would develop what's known as lockjaw. You'd be unable to open your jaw wide. Pressure will have pushed against your body with such force that it's keeping it from functioning correctly. In fact, the hydrostatic pressure is so powerful that if a boat were to sink deep enough, at some point its metal would literally collapse. The pressure would crumple a several-ton boat like paper. That's why submarines are pressurized inside—to counterbalance the pressure coming from outside the boat. This allows them to sustain themselves in the pit of the darkness that consumes the deepest parts of the ocean, and certainly it's the only way submarines can safely get to the bottom.

The Holy Spirit's role is to counterbalance the pressure coming at you from the outside world. When you're close to the Spirit, you have a counterbalance within you that keeps you from crumpling under the weight of all around you.

Too few kingdom followers walk closely enough with the Holy Spirit to fully experience the impact of the internal pressurization He provides. His presence enables you to stay under the water as the storms rage around you, but if you're not connecting with His presence in any form, allowing your spirit to be swayed and influenced by all else around you, you'll eventually cave in to the pressure. Your world will crumple just like the world outside of Noah did so many years ago.

The Whispering Voice of a Loving God

The passage we looked at earlier—Genesis 6:1-7—told us Noah didn't give in to the world's pressure. He lived a blameless life in the midst of a crooked culture. He didn't just go to church. Rather, he walked with God. As a result, God spared Noah and his family from the global disaster that came. In fact, in Hebrews 11:7 we see that God even "warned" Noah ahead of time so he could prepare for it. He let Noah in on what was to come.

Wouldn't it be nice if we could know what is to come? Wouldn't it make life a whole lot less stressful if we could prepare for things because we knew they were to take place? Noah had the luxury of having enough time to plan ahead because God gave him a forewarning of the disaster at hand.

I feel for the Christians who spend their lives without ever hearing the voice of God. I feel for those who have never experienced God speaking to their thoughts and bringing ideas to their minds or creating circumstances to guide them. Life is hard enough as it is. But to go through life without the whispering voice of a loving God in your ear is aimless at best and disastrous at worst.

Noah heard the voice of God, and he took what God said to heart. He got busy. He followed God's direction as recorded for us in Genesis 6.

> God said to Noah, "The end of all flesh has come before Me; for the earth is filled with violence because of them; and behold, I am about to destroy them with the earth. Make for yourself an ark of gopher wood; you shall make the ark with rooms, and shall cover it inside and out with pitch" (verses 13-14).

Just Do It—All of It

God continued His conversation with Noah, giving him detailed instructions for how to build this thing for weather the world had never seen: rain. Then Noah got to work. He set out to do what had never been done. He'd never even seen a flood. Up to this point, the earth had received water only one way—out of the ground. So of course the concept of rain was new to him. Not only that, but Noah lived a hundred miles away from an ocean, and he didn't have a truck or trailer to haul the ark to deep water once it was built. But none of that stopped Noah from doing what needed to be done. God had told him to do it, and that was all he needed to know.

I'm sure Noah's neighbors talked about him during this building project. I'm sure he was the brunt of all jokes at the local eatery. I imagine as the years dragged on and Noah's boat got bigger, his reputation of being the weird guy on Ark Avenue spread near and far. But that's what can happen when you walk so close to God that He gives you His secrets.

Keep in mind, when God is able to speak to you about what He plans to do directly, and He asks you to take part in it, what He asks of you will often appear weird to the world. In fact, how weird it seems to others usually reflects how big what God is going to do is about to get.

Noah built a boat on dry land—a structure roughly one and half football fields in length and four stories high. He spent 120 years doing it, which is exactly why God picked him in the first place. Genesis 6:22 gives us the blueprint for a kingdom hero when it says, "Thus Noah did; according to all that God had commanded him, so he did."

That's the definition of a kingdom hero in three words: *Thus Noah did.* He did it. What's more, he did all of it. That half-built ark we saw when we walked into Noah's exhibit now towers in front of us as we enter an enormously expansive space where an exact replica of the finished ark sits. Noah finished the job. Every single thing God commanded him to do, he did. It was a huge task, but he completed it.

Noah's story is a reminder to all of us: When God asks us to do something, we should do it. All of it. Even if it seems weird. Even if it doesn't quite make sense. Even if it takes us off the beaten path of normative culture. Obedience is the key to activating our faith as a kingdom hero. Without obedience, faith remains conceptual at best. To walk by faith involves completing all God tells us to do, not just some of it. It includes fulfilling all the work He's placed us here to fulfill. Noah exercised faith when he went out and chopped down the first gopher wood tree. And he continued exercising faith each and every day for the next 120 years.

I don't know this for sure, but I imagine there had to be days when Noah got tired of chopping down trees. Moments when he got weary of piecing together wood into the shape of something he'd never even seen before. Yet even though he may have grown tired and weary, he never quit. He pushed through. Kept going. And he made God's name known in the process. In fact, 2 Peter 2:5 says that, on top of being a boat builder, Noah was a preacher. We read that God "did not spare the ancient world, but preserved Noah, a preacher of righteousness, with seven others, when He brought a flood upon the world of the ungodly."

Noah may have had only had one sermon in his pocket, but he knew it well: "Repent. It's going to rain." Noah worked, and he witnessed. Like Enoch before him in the Hall of Heroes, he proclaimed his faith. He was not a secret agent Christian or a spiritual CIA representative. Noah was not an undecided voter. He believed in the power of God and preached about that power to others. Kingdom heroes do no less.

In other words, if you were accused of being a follower of Jesus Christ in your work, would there be enough evidence to convict you? Or would you be found innocent of all charges? With Noah, everyone knew. It was crystal clear where he stood. Proclaiming God was simply how Noah rolled.

What's more, he rolled like that in reverence. As we read earlier in Hebrews 11:7, "In reverence [Noah] prepared an ark for the salvation of his household," Noah didn't take his role lightly. He didn't take his job for granted. He worshipped as he worked. He praised as he chopped down gopher wood trees. He honored God with his heart as he sawed the wood into pieces that could fit together to make a structure. Noah gave God glory as he applied the pitch to keep the water out of the boat. And in the midst of a pagan, demonically infiltrated, pleasure-ridden, and violent culture, Noah lowered his head and worked with reverence. As a result, he not only saved himself but his family as well.

Isn't that the job of a kingdom hero—to save their family? The role of any kingdom hero is to position their family for spiritual victory, which is exactly what Noah did. Kingdom heroes don't walk away from their families. They don't abandon their homes. They don't leave their families to fend for themselves. Kingdom heroes look after the needs of their own.

Now, that doesn't mean your kids will grow up and choose righteousness. We know one of Noah's children wound up being cursed due to his own sin. But when you seek your family's welfare as a kingdom man or kingdom woman, it positions your family for spiritual success. Whether they live it out is up to them. But at least you've given them the opportunity.

Noah walked so closely with God that his actions spoke as loudly as his words. How many of us can say that about our lives? Noah "condemned the world" by his work and his worship. His entire lifestyle preached a message of righteousness—rightly following God and aligning under His rule. Even though he didn't know how all the animals would get on the boat or how the boat would find its way to water, Noah did what he could where he was with what he had, because that's what God told him to do.

Friend, until God shows you how He plans to pull off the miraculous in your life, just do what He says to do. When it comes time to bring about a miracle or heroic move, He'll be there. He won't be late. He's prepared. Your obedience to what He tells you to do right now will position you to receive His intervention and assistance when it's needed the most. If you're from Missouri and need God to "show" you how things will work out before you take your first step of faith, you won't have a boat when the tide rises or the oceans roll in. God isn't a *show you* kind of God. He's a faithful God who requires each of us to walk in faith out of a heart that trusts in Him to keep His word.

Don't Wait, Move!

One of the reasons we don't see more of God in the unseen realms of our lives is that our feet aren't moving, or if they are, they're moving slowly, partially, or in the wrong direction.

I know the Christian life can be challenging. I realize some of you may want to call it a day. Maybe some of you even want to quit the good fight altogether. Maybe some of you singles are finding it hard to locate someone to date who doesn't seek to compromise your standards. Or maybe some of you have lost jobs or friends over standing up for what you believe. But whatever your situation may be, a day will come when God makes clear where He stands to everyone. And if you're walking with Him according to His plan at that time, you'll find yourself safe and secure in His everlasting care while the rebellious discover it's too late. The water has risen and the floods have come.

Noah lived in a time when the culture had gone left. But to be frank with you, we also live in a time when the culture has gone left. We're witnessing the days of Noah right before us. We're seeing demonic possession and demonic influence everywhere. We're experiencing the compromise of virtues and kingdom values as a society at large. Even many within the church are rebelling against God.

The Bible tells us when we see days like these, we're to look up and keep watch for God. Luke 21:28 puts it like this: "When these things begin to take place, straighten up and lift up your heads, because your redemption is drawing near."

I used to enjoy watching a TV show called *Early Edition*. The main character somehow got tomorrow's paper delivered a day ahead, enabling him to see the news of tomorrow in advance. As a result, he could do things to bring about change that positively impacted outcomes. If an accident was reported in the paper, he tried to prevent it from happening. He brought about a lot of good simply by knowing about the bad about to take place, a day ahead of time.

Noah didn't get the newspaper delivered to him, but he did know what was coming tomorrow. So he walked in light of that today. He made his decisions based on what he knew about the future so that when the negative events of the future transpired, he was well prepared and safe.

You and I don't specifically know the future, but we've been given an opportunity to position ourselves and our families for a better tomorrow by what we do today. We gain access to a greater use of this opportunity when we walk closely with God, cleanse our own lives of any and all unrighteousness through the forgiveness of our sins through the atonement of Jesus Christ, and obey what God has told us to do. As we do these things, we position ourselves, both individually and collectively, to usher in our own safe passage when the storms of this world roll in.

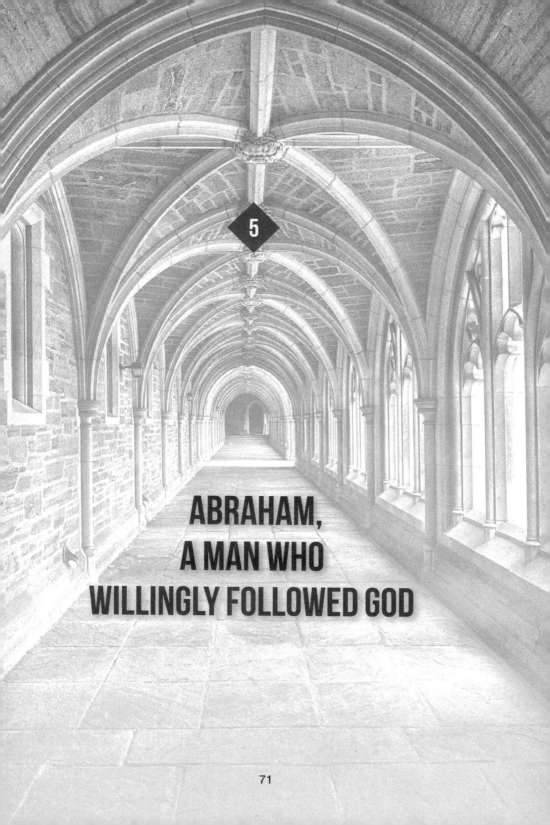

5

ABRAHAM, A MAN WHO A MAN WHO WILLINGLY FOLLOWED GOD

Only two ways to live your life exist. One is by sight. The other is by faith.

If you live by sight and not by faith, it's impossible to please God. If you're not pleasing God, then His involvement with you is limited because He responds to faith. He responds to people who believe in His integrity—people who know He's not lying and who will operate based on His words even though they don't see the evidence with their physical senses.

Remember, faith is acting like God is telling the truth even when it might be so simply because God said so. It all depends on you making decisions based on what God said even though you don't yet see the fruition of what He said in the visible, physical realm.

As we walk through the Hall of Heroes together, we continue to learn from each person's display in order to gain insight into kingdom qualities that can produce heroic actions in our own lives as well. We've learned that Abel worshipped by faith. Enoch walked by faith. Noah worked by faith. And as we continue on our journey, we'll next discover that Abraham, who began life with the name Abram, went out by faith.

As we are about to enter Abraham's exhibit, we first see these words written on the wall directly in front of us. They're taken from Hebrews 11:8-10.

> By faith Abraham, when he was called, obeyed by going out to
> a place which he was to receive for an inheritance; and he went
> out, not knowing where he was going. By faith he lived as an
> alien in the land of promise, as in a foreign land, dwelling in
> tents with Isaac and Jacob, fellow heirs of the same promise; for
> he was looking for the city which has foundations, whose archi-
> tect and builder is God.

In this kingdom hero exhibit, we discover three important things about
Abraham's walk of faith, which, if you apply them in your life, will enable
you to experience God at a whole new level. These three things involved
Abraham leaving, living, and looking.

Why We Leave

Abraham began his journey by leaving, by going out from where he'd
been living all of his life when God told him to go. This is also described
for us in Genesis 12:1-4:

> The LORD said to Abram, "Go forth from your country, and from
> your relatives and from your father's house, to the land which I
> will show you; and I will make you a great nation, and I will bless
> you, and make your name great; and so you shall be a blessing;
> and I will bless those who bless you, and the one who curses you I
> will curse. And in you all the families of the earth will be blessed."
> So Abram went forth as the LORD had spoken to him; and Lot
> went with him. Now Abram was seventy-five years old when he
> departed from Haran.

To understand why God would be calling a 75-year-old man to leave
the land he was raised in, the land of his history, we need to go back a chapter and look at Genesis 11. There, we discover a similar cultural situation to
Noah's. The whole world had rebelled against God. A man named Nim-
rod had led an insurrection against God's rule on earth, and most everyone had followed him. The Tower of Babel had established the religion of
humanism when people gathered to construct a man-centered civilization
apart from God. In fact, they sought to erect their tower high enough to

penetrate the heavens. They'd chosen to come together on one common ground—opposition to God. Their progressions as a society in the areas of intelligence, science, and technology had caused them to feel as if they were ready to live independently of the Source of their own creation.

Of course, they were wrong.

God looked upon the people uniting to mutiny on earth and came down to address their rebellion. Now, keep in mind, if God "comes down" to address something a group of people is building to reach up to Him, He's obviously much larger and much higher than anything anyone could set up.

God saw that, rather than taking His name, they'd sought to make a name for themselves. They'd sought to draw the worship away from Him and toward themselves. So He intervened. He scrambled their language, thus thwarting their ability to communicate. He also "scattered them abroad over the face of the whole earth" (Genesis 11:6-9).

Abraham's call to leave his home region and set out for someplace new came in the context of this attempt at worldwide paganism. Not only that, but Abraham's own family and heritage ran rife with idol worship as well. We read this in Joshua 24:2:

> Joshua said to all the people, "Thus says the LORD, the God of Israel, 'From ancient times your fathers lived beyond the River, namely, Terah, the father of Abraham and the father of Nahor, and they served other gods.'"

Abraham had been raised in a culture of chaos and a family intent on worshipping false gods.

Now, for God to carry out His purpose and destiny for Abraham's life, He first had to extract him from everything he'd ever known. But God wasn't going to show Abraham where He was taking him until he first left where he was. Again, in Genesis 12:1, God tells Abraham to go "to the land which I will show you."

The same often holds true for us. God will not take us to our destiny and the fulfillment of the promises He has for us until we're willing to leave what we know. We can't stay around paganism and still have God. We can't hang out with humanism and still have God. In order to live out the full realization of our divine reality, We have to trust that God knows where He's taking us even though He doesn't always tell us where that is.

Far too many of us instead choose to approach God like this:

> God, show me where You're taking me, and then I'll let You know if I'm going. Show me where You want me to be, and then I'll decide if I'll take that trip. But first, I want You to lay out the whole thing in an itinerary, giving me a look at each step of the journey and what I can expect.

But that's called walking by sight. If you have sight, then it's not faith at all. God doesn't show you what's going to happen each step of the way. In fact, He might not even show you where He's taking you. Instead, He asks you to trust Him all along the way. Abraham had to leave the worldliness that surrounded him before he could reach the destiny God had for him. We are to do no less.

First John 2:15 puts it this way: "Do not love the world nor the things in the world. If anyone loves the world, the love of the Father is not in him." To put it another way, anyone who is friends with the world is an enemy of God.

God has called each of us to leave worldliness behind. Now, that doesn't mean we're to cease to exist in society. No, in fact, we have responsibilities to carry out if we're to influence the culture for good. But God has called each of us to leave the world's philosophies, beliefs, attitudes, and actions behind. We'll never know where God is taking us unless we're willing to leave where we are. Abraham knew this to be true. Thus, he was willing to set out on a new journey at such a late stage in his life.

Of course, God motivated Abraham to leave by letting him know He had an inheritance for him. As we saw earlier, Abraham left his known land in order to gain something new. Similarly, God has an inheritance for you that involves your destiny. He has a purpose and a plan for you to fulfill. But God will not show you your destiny if He can't get you to first leave where you're stuck. As long as you're hanging out with the world and its values, entertainment systems, priorities, and more, you're at odds with God. God cannot communicate with you when you have the world's "music" blaring all around you.

Have you ever rented a condo or hotel room only to have the quiet, serene vacation or respite you'd hoped for deteriorate into a noisy, loud, distraction of a time? This can happen when others decide to play their music more loudly and for longer periods than what's reasonable for everyone else. Or they choose to be loud with their voices and laughter and partying to such a degree that the noise seeps through the walls, windows, and doors. The clamor and clang of the world's "songs" compete with the communion you'd hoped to have with God and your friends or family in choosing a beautiful spot.

Our lives are little different. You won't get to hear heaven talk, or receive answers to your prayers, or take advantage of any direction and guidance given if you can't tune out the world's competing songs. It will all simply blend together into a cacophony of not much more than sheer noise. Even Jesus sought to get away to a quiet place when He wanted to commune with the Father. Hearing from God and knowing what it means to live out your destiny as a kingdom hero requires the quieting of all competing voices, even if you once enjoyed them.

After all, Abraham wasn't living a despairing life when God called him out. He wasn't down to his last dime. He wasn't just trying to make it or get by. He wasn't depressed. No, the Bible tells us Abraham was prosperous. His home was where his businesses thrived. It's where his friends were. It's where his reputation had taken root and spread. I'm sure it wasn't an easy decision for him to just cut all ties and move on to the beat of a new tune. But his journey came as a result of his faith. He'd heard the voice of God and had obeyed it, leaving everything he'd once known and enjoyed for the pursuit of a greater inheritance.

If you really want to experience God's inheritance made real in your life, you have to decide if the new thing He has for you is more important than what you currently have.

When I was growing up in Baltimore, I spent hours playing marbles. That game was the in-thing to do, and over time, I got very good at it. For those of you who've never played, you put your marbles in a circle and then try to pop them out of the circle with another marble. As I gained more and more experience, I was able to move farther back from the circle and yet still knock out my marbles. In fact, one time, when I was roughly six feet back from the circle, I aimed my marble so accurately that when I hit the marble I was going for, it cracked the marble in half!

Playing marbles was fun. But as I grew into my teen years, something happened. Someone handed me a football. After discovering the game of football and how much I enjoyed playing it, my passion for marbles waned. I spent less and less time playing marbles while investing more and more time playing football. Eventually, I chose to say good-bye to marbles altogether. My new direction had taken me from my old ways.

When handed a heavenly football, far too many believers simply shrug it off and go back to playing marbles. They fail to pursue something new. They refuse to step out of the comfort zone of already being great at something to learn a new skill or discover a new passion in life. They stay stuck in the rut of religious ritual rather than releasing their inner kingdom hero. Unless a person truly believes God has a destiny for them that is so spectacular, powerful, potent, and purposeful so as to blow their minds, they'll stick with marbles. They'll be satisfied with staying in the circle of a safe and predictable life.

Here's the question: Do you love the world so much that you're willing to lose your destiny for it? God knows where He wants to take you, but you must be willing to leave some of what you know best in order to step out in faith and follow Him.

For some of you, that may mean saying good-bye to a worldly relationship that's keeping you from living a faith-filled, heroic life. For others, it might mean leaving a worldly scenario like when the guys or ladies go out together after work and aren't up to much good. Some of you may lose a friendship or need to leave old dreams behind. Whatever God is asking you to release in order for Him to bring about His full work in your life, you need to let it go. If you don't, you'll wind up stuck "playing marbles."

Unless you leave the old, you will never discover what God has for you in the new. Do you want Him and His plan for you? Or do you want the world's plans for you? You get to choose. Actually, you have to choose because you can't have both. Even not choosing is choosing. It's choosing the world. A life of faith requires a leaving of worldliness, wrong desires, words, and actions in conflict with God.

How We Live

Your life of faith as a kingdom hero will also involve how you choose to live. Earlier, we read in Hebrews 11:9 that "by faith [Abraham] lived as an alien in the land of promise, as in a foreign land, dwelling in tents with Isaac and Jacob, fellow heirs of the same promise." First, Abraham left what he knew, and then he chose to live as a stranger in a foreign land. He lived as an alien in the midst of a promise yet to be fulfilled. Abraham didn't march straight into his destiny. Rather, he wandered into a holding pattern of sorts. He made it to the area promised to him, but it was not yet his.

Perhaps no discipline in the kingdom hero's toolbox of faith is greater than the discipline of waiting well. Far too many people forfeit their destinies simply because they bail out during the waiting. They make it to the vicinity of their victory but give up before they grasp it. It's easy to do, but just because you're close doesn't mean you've captured it yet. Close doesn't count when it comes to living out your purpose.

One time I was flying for a speaking engagement when the pilot came on the plane's address system to let us know bad weather had developed where we were headed. Because of the storms near the airport, he'd been asked to fly in a holding pattern. Now, this concerned me. If I didn't get to my destination on time to speak, those in attendance could be confused and concerned. I didn't want to let them down. But regardless of my own plans, someone in the cockpit of the plane I sat in—someone I couldn't even see—informed me that the time I'd expected to arrive was no longer valid. Until the weather system passed through, I was stuck. Not only that, but I was stuck indefinitely.

Now, I was in the vicinity of where I wanted to go, but I still wasn't quite able to make it. I was close, but close wasn't good enough. Some of you may be feeling like this right now. You feel like you're stopped at a red light that will never turn green. Or like when you're in the waiting room at your physician's office with a receptionist who keeps telling you the doctor is coming but that never happens. You hear footsteps in the hallway and your heart starts to beat a little faster from hope, but then the footsteps walk by. You sigh.

I know how waiting feels as well as anyone. When I was stuck on that plane and we finally got permission to land, my spirit lifted. I thought I would make it to the event on time after all. But once we landed, the same pilot told us no gates were available for us, so we had to wait once again, on the tarmac for an indefinite amount of time. Sometimes it can feel harder to wait for something when you're close to it. If it seems far off in the distance, you can set your thoughts aside and keep your emotions calm. But when it's close—when you can almost reach out and touch it—the desire to have it increases all the more.

Abraham had made it to the land God sent him to seek out. But when he arrived, he was placed in a holding pattern. He was asked to live as a stranger in a strange land rather than set up camp and call it *home*. Abraham lived in a tent called promise while waiting for the promise to come about.

When you're in a holding pattern for His promise, God is doing two things related to your life at once. First, He's preparing the promise for you, and second, He's preparing you for the promise. Whatever your inheritance, destiny, or purpose may be, He has to get it ready before you walk into it. But more than that, He has to get you ready to handle it wisely once you get it.

Many millionaires who won their money playing the lottery have lost it nearly as quickly as it came. If you're not prepared to know how to make wise choices with the blessings given to you, once you get those blessings you can easily lose your purpose and destiny through your own wrong choices. That being so, God seeks to prepare you so you won't mess up.

Now, you have no control over how God is preparing the promise for you (the people, places, and purpose), but you can control how quickly it takes to prepare you for the promise. If you're in a holding pattern, that doesn't mean God couldn't have your inheritance ready for you right now. It means He's still waiting for you to mature to the point where you won't lose it as fast as you get it. If you're still looking back at the world like Lot's wife did, then He doesn't arrange for your promise to come about.

It's sobering to realize this, but it's true: Most people delay the promise they're waiting for because they choose not to wait well. They choose not to cooperate with the learning of the lessons and the spiritual growth God has for them in the interim.

That's what happened to Abraham. He ended up in the Hall of Heroes, but not every decision he made was heroic. Due to some very bad choices, he delayed his breakthrough to his first promise by some 25 years. It would be that long before his son of promise, Isaac, would be born. Abraham wasn't ready. He was still lying, cheating, and even sleeping with his wife's handmaiden, resulting in a baby being born outside of God's will. Abraham needed some development before he got his inheritance. He first needed to come to his senses, grow in his faith, and trust God fully—even when it didn't look like anything was happening.

God never wants to give someone a destiny that will cause them to forget Him when they get it. But that's one of the problems we face with everyone running around looking for their blessing. It's all about them. Or they're looking for God to rescue them from a situation, promising to follow Him if He will just get them out of their bind. But truth be told, those promises last a week or two at most. When God delivers on those promises, we often praise Him and then just as quickly forget He did. We forget because we lack the kind of commitment that's tied to more than what we see and what we get.

Abraham lived for a very long time as a foreigner in a strange land, in a tent as opposed to a permanent location while God moved him from place to place rather than settling him for good. We are to live as foreigners in a strange land as well. First Peter 2:11-12 puts it like this:

> Beloved, I urge you as aliens and strangers to abstain from fleshly lusts which wage war against the soul. Keep your behavior excellent among the Gentiles, so that in the thing in which they slander you as evildoers, they may because of your good deeds, as they observe them, glorify God in the day of visitation.

God doesn't want any of us to get too attached to the world we live in now. We aren't to adopt the culture so much that our behavior begins to reflect the common behaviors of the culture. Not only that, but due to the ever-revealing nature of God's relationship with each of us, remaining mobile frees us to pursue His plan more fully. If you're going to walk by faith, you better have on loafers or comfortable shoes, because God can take you on some long and winding paths. Staying tied too closely to your comfort zone will limit what God is able to do both in and through you.

When I stay in a hotel, I don't unpack my suitcase and put my clothes away in the drawers. Neither do I hang pictures of my family on the walls. I don't even organize my belongings in the bathroom much. I just put my bathroom kit on the counter to dig through as needed. That's because I'm just passing through. I have no intention to stay there much longer than one night or two. I certainly don't act like I live there by getting too comfortable, simply because I know I'm not staying.

Here's what God is trying to say to many of those who are in the Kingdom Hero Academy right now: If He's going to take you to your greatest feats and mightiest accomplishments found in His inheritance for you, keep your shoes on and your bags packed, because you're about to go through some stuff. Development for your destiny is never an easy path, just like developing your muscles is not an easy task. You'll encounter mountains to climb, valleys to go through, hills to hike, and waters to wade before all is said and done. Each of these struggles is designed to develop you so that, when you get to your destiny, you won't blow it. So when you get a spot on the kingdom hero roster, you will hold your own. What's more, you won't showboat your time, causing the morale of everyone else around you to go down.

By faith Abraham went through his trials, tests, and the learning curves of life. By faith he made his mistakes—lying, cheating, and so on—and grew in wisdom. He did this all by faith because he was willing to live as a foreigner in a strange land while he waited on God to change his scenario and mature his heart.

Some of us are coming up on 50 years of things that should have been solved in three years because we've built a house though God asked us to merely pitch a tent. We put down roots when He asked us to move out. If God doesn't have flexibility with our lives so He can grow us like He wants to, we'll stay stuck in a rut of routine, waiting on Him to change things while He's waiting on us to change. We'll wind up like a mouse on a wheel, working as hard as we can to get nowhere at all.

Where We Look

Abraham wanted his inheritance. He wanted the fulfillment of the destiny God had promised him. But he wasn't perfect; he had his flaws. Yet when he was knocked down, he got back up and started over. He didn't pitch a fit when God told him to pitch his tent in a new location. Why? Because he had his eye on the prize. He had his sights set high. He was looking for "the city which has foundations, whose architect and builder is God" (Hebrews 11:10).

Abraham left the world of his comfort zone, living in the arena of the promise but remaining fluid enough to grow and develop as the circumstances entailed. He knew that before deliverance could be given to him, he had to be developed for his destiny. The way he survived that long season was in his focus. He chose to look at where he was going rather than where he had been. He looked for the city whose designer and builder was God. In short, he looked toward heaven.

If and when you learn to look toward heaven, you'll live better on earth. But if you stop looking toward heaven and focus only on what's taking place on earth, you'll miss out on the rewards of both. This is because, in earth's environment, we cannot see clearly. We can't discern the spiritual without the help of the Spirit. As the apostle Paul put it, "Now we see in a mirror dimly, but then face to face; now I know in part, but then I will know fully just as I also have been fully known" (1 Corinthians 13:12).

Kingdom heroes are to view all of life from an eternal perspective. That doesn't mean we become so heavenly minded that we're no longer any earthly good. But it does mean we integrate heaven's perspective into all of our life on earth. We bring God's rule, His thoughts, and His will to bear on our decisions, words, and values as we pursue an intimate relationship with Him.

This world is passing away, so you never want to hinge your whole life to its wagon. It will soon be gone, and you will soon be gone from it. Time goes by like a vapor, and before you know it, your life will be nearing its end. This world, at best, is temporary. In order to navigate through the various footpaths and trails of this life, you must do so with an eternal focus. Because when you lose sight of heaven, your perspective will be ruined on earth. Your life will become only about what you have here, experience now, or have to worry about in the future. In short, you will live lost.

There must be a shift in your perspective to fully experience your life and what it's meant to be. This shift will enable you to handle life's challenges with grace. It will give you the strength and wisdom to go through life's difficulties with dignity. This is because you will know that nothing will come to you that doesn't first pass through God's sovereign, purposeful, and loving hand. When you trust His heart, you don't have to understand His hand.

When my son Anthony was young, he suffered from asthma, and when an attack set in, I'd take him to the ER when necessary. But if I had the opportunity to take him to Dr. Denny, his primary doctor, I would. Dr. Denny was a very wise man.

As Anthony sat on my lap wheezing or trying to get his breath, Dr. Denny would reach into a drawer and pull out a sucker (or lollipop for those of you in other parts of the country). Even though Anthony would be struggling to breathe, he would go for the candy every time. As he licked it, Dr. Denny would come around to Anthony's side and give him an epinephrine shot.

Initially, the sting in his arm drew Anthony's attention away from his treat, and he would let out a cry. He was not only in pain but felt faked out by the doctor and betrayed by his dad for taking him where a needle would be stuck into his arm. He looked at me with such a confused expression, wondering why his father, who said he loved him, would take him to a place of pain.

But it didn't take long for that pain to subside, and Anthony's eyes were drawn back to the sugary sweetness in his hand. With tears flowing down his face, he started licking that sucker again, and before he knew it, his perspective had changed. He was no longer crying. And he was no longer wheezing. The sweetness and the healing effect of the medicine took hold and impacted him more than the pain.

Anyone who's studied the lives of those found in the Hall of Heroes will notice one common theme between them all: pain. Their lives had struggles, disappointments, trials, issues, disturbances, and more. But they also knew where to look in their pain. Heavenward. They looked to God. They chose a kingdom perspective rather than an earthly view. As a result, they lived out the destinies they'd been created to fulfill. They experienced the accomplishments they knew deep in their hearts they could and would make. They walked with God as kingdom heroes in the midst of a world composed of villains and rogues.

Where you look determines where you wind up. You can't walk forward if you're looking behind. You can't live out greatness in your future if you're stuck staring at your past. I want to encourage you to, like Abraham, listen to God when He speaks to you. Leave when He tells you to go. Then, when you do, choose to live fully in the environment where He's placed you so you can learn the lessons He has for you to learn there.

And while you are, remember to keep your eyes on Him as He gives you the spiritual perspective you need to navigate the terrain in front of you. Kingdom heroes don't always know what's around the next corner or over the next hill, but one thing they do know—if they just keep walking according to the direction of their King, they will reach a glorious purpose and destiny.

SARAH, A WOMAN WHO WAITED WELL FOR GOD'S PROMISE

A woman lived far out in the hills of the country. In fact, she lived so far out that her home had no electricity, and she'd been living without it for many years. Then when her area finally got power, the electric company sent a representative to speak to the community's members, making sure they knew they had it and training them on how to use it.

After a few months, the electric company noticed this woman barely used any electricity. So they sent a repairman to see if there was a problem with the lines. When he didn't find one, he knocked on the woman's door.

"Ma'am," he said when she answered, "we've noticed you haven't been using much electricity, and I'm here to see if everything's all right."

"Yes, everything's fine," the woman replied. "I use the electricity every single night."

The repairman got a confused look on his face, so the woman explained. "I turn on my electric lamp when it's getting dark, allowing me to see better as I light my kerosene lamp. Then I turn it back off."

Obviously, this woman who'd lived without power for so long didn't understand what she now had at her disposal. She didn't understand how she could use the resource she'd been connected to. As a result, instead of maximizing the power available to her, she simply visited it and kept her old way of operating.

What you believe determines what you receive.

Our next exhibit in the Hall of Heroes illustrates this truth in dramatic fashion. This hero's name is Sarah. She started life as Sarai, and she married Abraham, who, again, began life as Abram. God renamed them both but at separate times. (Abraham also appears in the next couple of exhibits, so I guess we could call this the Abrahamic Wing.)

At the start of this exhibit, Scripture written on one wall tells us God promised both Sarah and Abraham a son. God did this the same time he changed Sarah's name:

> As for Sarai your wife, you shall not call her name Sarai, but Sarah shall be her name. I will bless her, and indeed I will give you a son by her (Genesis 17:15-16).

Now, the promise of a son doesn't seem like a big deal unless you take into account the potential parents' ages. By then, both Sarah and Abraham were advanced in years (Sarah was 90), neither of them still in the normal childbearing years. Not even close. So this promise from God simply didn't fit the facts of their lives. What He'd promised wasn't practical. What He'd declared didn't match reality. Not only was Sarah old, but she'd been barren her entire life. She'd never conceived or given birth to a child. Her physical capacity to do so was absent, and time was no longer on her side.

It's possible that Sarah's story resembles your own but in a different way. You could be barren in other forms. Your capacity to experience what God has for you just doesn't seem to be there. It's not working out. You're not producing what you thought you would be at this stage in your life. You're not delivering on the destiny you believed to be yours. You've heard Jesus' promise in John 10:10, when He declared. "I came that they may have life, and have it abundantly." But you don't see the results of that promise in your everyday life.

If that's you, you may be stuck in emotions of disappointment, despair, and little hope. These negative emotions then contribute to an inertia or lack of energy to keep trying, keep believing, and keep pursuing God's plan for your life.

If that describes your current state of mind, know that Sarah was right where you are. Five times God had told her she was going to have a son. Not only that, but He'd gone on to tell Abraham and her that, through this son, a whole nation would be birthed. Sarah had a vision for a great future. Yet the clock kept ticking, taunting her. Tempting her to give up and doubt God. Luring her into a mindset of lack.

If we were to look closely, we'd see that many of our lives look like this—like our ability to be what God wants us to be, to do what God wants us to do, and to achieve what God wants us to achieve no longer exists. The gap in time for those opportunities has closed entirely. Perhaps it's the single Christian who's lived an extended amount of time alone, and it looks like the possibility of marriage is no longer there. Or perhaps it's the person who merely punches in at work rather than expressing their passions and gifts through a career path more in line with their personality.

Whatever the case, if you feel like too much time has passed to get to experience the fulfillment of Christ's promise of the abundant and fulfilling life, I encourage you to never let the facts get in the way of your faith. Don't deny the facts—facts are facts—but just know that faith is never limited to facts alone. Facts always involve what you see. Faith involves what you don't see.

Many problems arise when facts conflict with faith. This is where you reach a danger point in your beliefs, because based on the facts, God doesn't seem to be working things out for you. When you examine His promises, both in His Word and with what the Holy Spirit has confirmed to your spirit, God doesn't seem to be bringing them about.

I'm sure Sarah felt her opportunity to bear a child had long been gone. Maybe if she were younger, she could still believe in the promise given. But at this point in her life—nearing 90—it was becoming a challenge to have any faith at all. Maybe she'd heard wrong. Maybe the promise had been contingent on something she or her husband had failed to do. Maybe God had changed His mind and forgotten to tell them.

Don't Try to Help God

These thoughts and more probably made their home in Sarah's heart, causing her to doubt the promise of new life. And we believe this is the case because of what she chose to do next. When the promise hadn't come about for an extended period of time, she decided to help God. She jumped in to manipulate the situation and sought to force the promise to take place.

The tendency to want to usher in God's promises on our own lies in all of us. As a result, we go outside of God in order to help Him. And that's exactly what Sarah did when she suggested her husband sleep with her handmaiden and perhaps have a child.

Now we enter the next section of the exhibit, where we see the figure of a beautiful young woman standing off by her tent. We also see a sculpture of a much older Sarah, whispering something to her aged husband. In between the two displays is a sign with these words from Genesis 16:1-4:

> Now Sarai, Abram's wife had borne him no children, and she had an Egyptian maid whose name was Hagar. So Sarai said to Abram, "Now behold, the LORD has prevented me from bearing children. Please go in to my maid; perhaps I will obtain children through her." And Abram listened to the voice of Sarai. After Abram had lived ten years in the land of Canaan, Abram's wife Sarai took Hagar the Egyptian, her maid, and gave her to her husband Abram as his wife. He went in to Hagar, and she conceived; and when she saw that she had conceived, her mistress was despised in her sight.

Here's when you know you're not operating in faith: When you're using human reason to manipulate a situation. When you're going outside of God's will to try to accomplish His will. God had told these two He would give them a child, but Sarah opted to get practical with God. She made a suggestion for how His promise could take place, seeing that she'd been barren her whole adult life and was now advanced in age. In essence, her logic took over.

Our logic can take over too. It's okay to admit it. Because sometimes it seems like God is taking too long. He's moving too slow, and there appears to be no practical way for what He said would happen to happen. So we start to reason and rationalize the situation by thinking maybe God needs a little help. We can even get to the point where we consider sinning to help God bring about His blessing. That's what Sarah did. She chose an unrighteous action for her husband—sexual intercourse with her handmaiden—in order to seek to bring about a righteous outcome. But Sarah was wrong.

Hagar gave birth to Ishmael, which led to the Arab and Israeli conflict that exists to this day. Not only that, but Ishmael's conception and birth led to Sarah's deep bitterness and resentment toward Hagar. In short, she got jealous of her husband's baby mama.

This illegitimate approach to bringing about God's promise involved the flesh, and anytime we involve the flesh, we invite everything associated with the flesh into the scenario. Negative emotions such as rage, envy, and pride are introduced when someone seeks to handle a situation according to the ways of the flesh. What's more, when we turn to the flesh in order to help God out, we also delay His promises for our life. He'll take a step back and wait, because we're clearly not ready to live as a kingdom hero in full faith.

So many of us experience a delay of God working and moving in our lives because we keep going back to the flesh. We keep merging human logic and human reasoning with God's Word. But like oil and water, they don't mix. The Bible calls the attempt to merge them "double-mindedness" (Psalm 119:113; James 1:8; 4:8). It means working both sides of the table at the same time. You may think you're speeding up the process by doing so, but you're really pushing the pause button. You're delaying your destiny due to a lack of faith tied to God's Word.

This far into her story, you might be wondering how Sarah wound up in the Hall of Heroes. It doesn't seem like she's living a life worthy of such an honor. But that's why Hebrews 11:11, which we'll read in a moment, is such an important verse. It reminds us that it's never too late to turn to God. It's never too late to become a kingdom hero. No person has made too many mistakes, committed too many sins, or gone too far left that they can't return to God and live a life of faith.

Sarah doubted, so she tried to bring God's promise about in her own way. She took matters into her own hands. Maybe she felt like she always had to be in control. Whatever the case, her lack of faith led to chaos. But her ability to learn from her mistakes led to honor, and that's what we read in Hebrews 11:11: "By faith even Sarah herself received ability to conceive, even beyond the proper time of life, since she considered Him faithful who had promised."

Don't Mock the "Ridiculous"

Sarah eventually discovered that, even though what God said did not compare to her reality, she could still trust Him by faith. But she didn't learn that lesson, the lesson of waiting well, overnight. In fact, even after nearly 25 years of waiting, she still hadn't fully learned this lesson. Neither had Abraham. We know this by their responses when God again told Abraham that Sarah would bear a son at that time in a year.

Turn around and look to your right, where you'll see Abraham standing outside a large tent. A bright, shining light appears in front of him. The story is told for us in both Genesis 17 and 18, and portions of those two chapters appear inscribed above the display.

From chapter 17:

> God said to Abraham, "As for Sarai your wife, you shall not call her name Sarai, but Sarah shall be her name. I will bless her, and indeed I will give you a son by her. Then I will bless her, and she shall be a mother of nations; kings of peoples will come from her." Then Abraham fell on his face and laughed, and said in his heart, "Will a child be born to a man one hundred years old? And will Sarah, who is ninety years old, bear a child?"... "But My covenant

I will establish with Isaac, whom Sarah will bear to you at this season next year" (Genesis 17:15-17,21).

In the second passage from chapter 18, we're told Sarah is "at the tent door," and in the tent we see her ear is pressed against the tent to listen.

> The LORD appeared to [Abraham] by the oaks of Mamre, while he was sitting at the tent door in the heat of the day. When he lifted up his eyes and looked, behold, three men were standing opposite him; and when he saw them, he ran from the tent door to meet them and bowed himself to the earth, and said, "My Lord, if now I have found favor in Your sight, please do not pass Your servant by...
>
> Then they said to him, "Where is Sarah your wife?" And he said, "There, in the tent." [The representative of the Lord] said, "I will surely return to you at this time next year; and behold, Sarah your wife will have a son." And Sarah was listening at the tent door, which was behind him. Now Abraham and Sarah were old, advanced in age; Sarah was past childbearing. Sarah laughed to herself, saying, "After I have become old, shall I have pleasure, my lord being old also?"
>
> And the LORD said to Abraham, "Why did Sarah laugh, saying, 'Shall I indeed bear a child, when I am so old?' Is anything too difficult for the LORD? At the appointed time I will return to you, at this time next year, and Sarah will have a son." Sarah denied it however, saying, "I did not laugh"; for she was afraid. And He said, "No, but you did laugh" (Genesis 18:1-3,9-15).

Just inside the tent door, we can see Sarah is covering her mouth so her laughter won't be heard. But why did she laugh? Because she was acutely aware of both her age and her husband's. Not only did she doubt her ability to get pregnant, but she doubted Abraham's ability to even try to get her pregnant. Written across the outside of the tent are her words: "After I have become old, shall I have pleasure, my lord being old also?"

That's a pretty straightforward question. Sarah assumed that even super-Viagra couldn't help Abraham now. By then both she and Abraham had given up on God and felt the promise of their creating a son together was a joke. God's promise had become ridiculous given their current ages and circumstances.

The representative of the Lord answered Sarah's question clearly, even though she probably meant it as rhetorical and for herself. As we just saw in the passage, he reminded Abraham and Sarah to have faith. His words—"Is anything too difficult for the Lord?"—appear on the next exhibit, inscribed across the tent again. It's the same tent, but Sarah is no longer laughing.

God's promise for Sarah may have been impossible given the facts. But He wasn't talking about the facts when He gave it. Remember, nothing is too difficult for the God who created the earth out of nothing. The messenger's sharp rebuke had caught Sarah off-guard, and she tried to cover her tracks, claiming she hadn't really laughed at all. She was afraid her lack of faith had revealed too much.

At this stage in the story, it's still difficult to discern how Sarah will wind up in the Hall of Heroes. After all, she's laughed at God's promises. She's outright questioned them. And she's offered a young woman to her husband for his pleasure and to "help" God. But, thankfully, God didn't give up on Sarah. Rather, He allowed her to learn a few more things in order to strengthen her faith so she would no longer struggle with doubt.

Developing Faith

We know God did this because we see the critical lessons Sarah learned between the time she laughed and the time she gave birth to Isaac, as recorded in Genesis 21. Between Genesis 18 (the laugh) and Genesis 21 (the birth), two cataclysmic events took place. The first was what happened in Sodom and Gomorrah. Through the destruction of these powerful and thriving cities, God demonstrated His power to Sarah and Abraham on a whole new level. They were able to witness God's Word coming to light in the reality in which they lived. They saw the destruction of these twin cities, but they also saw God deliver their nephew Lot from the demise. This first event demonstrated God's power and faithfulness.

The second event involved a king and a castle. Abraham and Sarah had traveled to an area known as Gerar shortly after the destruction of Sodom and Gomorrah. In Gerar, Abraham most likely began to feel threatened by those around him. It's possible he thought he might be killed so that the king could have his wife. So he decided to pull what I call a *punk move* by telling everyone Sarah was his sister.

Abraham's lie then opened a Pandora's box of unintended consequences. Even though Sarah was advanced in years, she was still very attractive—so much so that the king in the region to which they'd traveled sent for her to be taken into his harem once he'd heard she was Abraham's sister and not married.

We read about this in the next section of the exhibit. As you enter a new room, you see a large castle painted on the wall in front of you with glimpses into the rooms inside the castle. The first sign to your left sets the stage for the story:

> Abraham journeyed from there toward the land of the Negev, and settled between Kadesh and Shur; then he sojourned in Gerar. Abraham said of Sarah his wife, "She is my sister." So Abimelech king of Gerar sent and took Sarah (Genesis 20:1-3).

As you look closer, you recognize Sarah as one of the women with the harem inside the castle. Her face is drawn. She looks worried. Her heart feels betrayed by her husband, who had chosen to lie about her, presumably to save his own life. But just because Abraham didn't stand up for his wife didn't mean Sarah was left entirely on her own.

If you look toward the king's chambers painted within the castle, you'll see him sleeping on a glorious-sized bed. Above him is a bright light with sounds coming from it. This is God visiting the king in his dream and giving him the truth about Sarah. The words inscribed just below the light and above the king's bed tell us what happened.

> God came to Abimelech in a dream of the night, and said to him, "Behold, you are a dead man because of the woman whom you

have taken, for she is married." Now Abimelech had not come near her; and he said, "Lord, will You slay a nation, even though blameless? Did he not himself say to me, 'She is my sister'? And she herself said, 'He is my brother.' In the integrity of my heart and the innocence of my hands I have done this."

Then God said to him in the dream, "Yes, I know that in the integrity of your heart you have done this, and I also kept you from sinning against Me; therefore I did not let you touch her. Now therefore, restore the man's wife, for he is a prophet, and he will pray for you and you will live. But if you do not restore her, know that you shall surely die, you and all who are yours" (Genesis 20:3-7).

As if Sarah's ultimate release and return to her husband wasn't enough to develop her faith, what happened next sealed the deal for her to be able to wait on her promise of bearing a son in full faith. When the king restored Sarah to her husband and gave gifts of vindication to Abimelech, since he had not known she was married, Abraham forgave Abimelech and prayed for him just as God had said. But what happened as a result of that prayer opened Sarah's eyes.

To the right of the castle, painted on the wall, are images of a smiling king and a harem of women holding babies standing behind him. Above them it says,

> Abraham prayed to God, and God healed Abimelech and his wife and his maids, so that they bore children. For the LORD had closed fast all the wombs of the household of Abimelech because of Sarah, Abraham's wife (verses 17-18).

God had shut the wombs of all of the women in Abimelech's kingdom due to Sarah's captivity. He wouldn't let anyone get pregnant until Sarah was released. But when she was released, He reopened the wombs of the women in Abimelech's land. That showed Sarah that God has the power to both close and open wombs. When young, healthy women couldn't bear children because God said so, and then suddenly they were able to bear children because God said so, that said an awful lot about God.

When God revealed His power on a national scale with Sodom and Gomorrah, Sarah witnessed His strength firsthand. She saw Him strike down the twin cities because of their sinful rebellion, yet all the while preserving Lot and his children. She then witnessed God close up the wombs of every woman in the land where she'd been taken into captivity by the king, then saw Him reopen those wombs.

God had allowed Sarah to see enough of His hand moving in external situations around her to strengthen her faith, to believe Him for the impossible situation within her. Often, God will do the same for you when He sees your faith continuing to decline as you wait on Him to move. He will reveal the strength of His might through other people's testimonies and lives.

That's why it's critical that kingdom followers make meeting together regularly a habit. Without ongoing fellowship and communion, we miss out on opportunities to hear how God is working in other people's lives. Small groups aren't just designed for group-based Bible study; they're also designed to allow believers the opportunity to hear from one another. We gain encouragement as we observe what God is doing for them.

Sarah's faith grew as she witnessed God's movement in the lives of those around her. In fact, it grew so much that she learned how to let go. She let go of her logic. She let go of her mocking laughter. She let go of the need to control the situation. When she let go and let God bring about the fruition of His promise in His right time and according to His perfect plan and in His prescribed way, Sarah experienced her miracle. We read about this in Genesis 21:

> Then the LORD took note of Sarah as He had said, and the LORD did for Sarah as He had promised. So Sarah conceived and bore a son to Abraham in his old age, at the appointed time of which God had spoken to him. Abraham called the name of his son who was born to him, whom Sarah bore to him, Isaac. Then Abraham circumcised his son Isaac when he was eight days old, as God had commanded him. Now Abraham was one hundred

years old when his son Isaac was born to him. Sarah said, "God has made laughter for me; everyone who hears will laugh with me." And she said, "Who would have said to Abraham that Sarah would nurse children? Yet I have borne him a son in his old age" (verses 1-7).

You've heard the saying *He who laughs last laughs best*. The last laugh is always the one that remains. In Sarah's case, she and God shared this laugh together. In fact, the name Isaac literally means "laughter."

Why does God put us in a situation that seems hopeless? So that when He does what He wants to do, only He gets the glory. God allows us to hit rock bottom so we'll discover that He is the Rock at the bottom. He may not change your scenario or your struggle until He sees you are waiting well within it. To wait well as a kingdom hero is to not go outside of God's prescribed ways in order to bring something about. It also means waiting with hope and expectation, not sarcastic doubt. The first time we saw Sarah laughing, she was mocking the promise God had given her. But the second time she laughed, it was out of awe at God's ability to pull off the impossible.

Sometimes God puts your back up against the wall, not to be mean but to let you see He is truly God. Sarah had to grow and mature to the point of waiting well. She made mistakes along the way. We all do. But the good news is that even if you've made mistakes, and even if you have your own set of Ishmaels running around as a result, it's never too late for God to intervene. Sarah had made a mess of things. Then to make matters worse, Abraham had gone and lied—making even more of a mess of things. Yet once they both witnessed God's power to both close and open wombs, they discovered just who they were dealing with.

Beware Division and Blame

In the next section of the exhibit, we see a larger-than-life sculpture displaying a very happy Abraham and a glowing Sarah holding their smiling baby boy. In order for this miracle to have taken place, both Sarah and Abraham had to believe.

We read these words inscribed on a rock near the family of three:

> Therefore there was born even of one man, and him as good as dead at that, as many descendants as the stars of heaven in number, and innumerable as the sand which is by the seashore (Hebrews 11:12).

As you can see, this verse reminds us that Abraham was "as good as dead" by the time he became the father of Isaac. God had to fix two people's barren situations in order to keep His promise. Sarah and Abraham didn't get Sarah pregnant on their own. What this emphasizes is that God often works with the two people in a marriage as one entity. This is such a critical point to explore, because Satan will often seek to divide a couple in order to prevent God's promises from taking root.

Not only did Sarah have to have an egg that would flow and receive the seed of her husband, but her husband also had to have seed that would flow. Both things had to happen. Both of them had been out of the will of God by mocking Him earlier with their laughter. Both had been out of God's will by lying about the true nature of their relationship in Gerar. Neither of them believed God too much at that point, but He was able to turn both their hearts toward Him by demonstrating His power through the closing and opening of other women's wombs.

As long as the devil can keep couples divided from each other and doubting God, he can keep the fulfillment of the spiritual promise of abundant life—and much more—from bearing fruit. The miraculous presence of God's promises are put on hold when a married couple lacks faith. The problem in most marriages today is that the two stay two rather than becoming one flesh. But unity is necessary for God to deliver on His promises, especially when it relates to a married couple.

Sarah had learned the skill of waiting well in faith, which ultimately produced her miracle. But in 1 Peter 3:6 we see she'd learned that part of waiting well in faith involves respecting and honoring those around you: "Sarah obeyed Abraham, calling him lord, and you have become her children if you do what is right without being frightened by any fear." In this verse, we see the respect Sarah showed specifically refers to her husband. But it doesn't have to be just toward a spouse. Anytime you or I are in a position where God has asked us to wait on His promises, believing He will bring them about, we are to do so in a way that honors others.

Far too often, blame comes to town when things don't go according to our own plans or timetables. In our frustration or disappointment, we might blame our spouse. Or we could blame a coworker or boss. Some people blame their parents for something that happened decades ago. Others blame a friend. Whatever the situation, blame has no place in a kingdom hero's heart. Part of waiting well in faith involves living according to the highest rule in the kingdom—the rule of love. First Corinthians 13:7 says love "bears all things, believes all things, hopes all things, endures all things." In short, love doesn't blame.

When Sarah stopped trying to solve the problem herself and blaming her husband for being too old, she got her miracle. When she stopped calling the shots in her marriage, she got her miracle. We know she was calling the shots because Abraham had become a passive husband in following her agenda to impregnate Hagar. All hell broke loose in their home because Sarah had stepped out of place and Abraham had cooperated with it.

But Peter reminds us that when Sarah called Abraham "lord," meaning she reverenced him with her words and honored him with her heart rather than bossing him with both, she got what she desired most. She got her son. What's more, Scripture tells us Sarah didn't die until she was 127 years old. She had her son at 90 years old. That means she got to be with Isaac for 37 years. She got to experience the joy of the family she'd always hoped for.

Peter tells us that if we follow the example of Sarah, honoring those we are to honor and waiting well in faith, we get to live without fear. We get to let go of our worries about the future that make us think we're too far gone to ever enjoy the promises of God even if He were to give them. When you align your heart under God and His rule and live according to the principles of kingdom heroes, you'll not only receive the fruition of the promises of God in your life but have the time to enjoy them.

God Gives Us Time

Through the life of this hero of the faith, we learn that we're never too old to hope in God. We're never too far gone to just give up. If you will place your faith in Him and His promises for your life, even if most of your life has already taken place, God can still give you His promises.

Not only that, but He can give you enough days, weeks, years, and even decades to enjoy His promises. Sarah is the only woman in the Bible whose age at death is given. God wanted to emphasize her years to point out He gave her time after giving her His promise of a son. She had 37 years with Isaac.

As you've grown older, I realize some of you single Christians reading this book might have had the thought cross your mind that you're wasting your life, that you're wasting the years you wanted to have with a spouse and family. You may even feel like there won't be anyone worthwhile left for you to marry at this stage in life. But I want to remind you that when God comes through for us with His blessings, like He did for Sarah, He can also give us the years to enjoy them. Nothing is too hard for God.

Or some of you may be midway through life, having invested most of your adult years in caring for a family, yet feel you still have personal dreams deep within. But you believe it's too late for those dreams. You may believe it's too late to enter a career field of your hopes and make something of it. Maybe you look at your résumé and wonder how you could ever attain the career you desire.

If you're wondering if it's too late, I want to assure you that when God is in the equation and you learn the skill of waiting well—waiting in faith with a heart of hope, surrender, and honor—God can not only bring about your promises and your dreams but bring them suddenly. You don't have to climb a career ladder when God is involved. He can usher you straight into where you're supposed to be if you'll look to Him to do it according to His will and His ways. He will do this if you look to Him in faith.

As we travel through this Hall of Heroes, I want you to understand who you're dealing with when it comes to God. Nothing is too hard for God to pull off, whenever He chooses to do it. The problems and the delays come about when we block Him from doing what He wants to do. He's waiting on us to exhibit our faith in a way that pleases Him.

As a reminder, faith is never just about your emotions. Faith demonstrates itself in tangible, concrete ways that reveal how much you trust God. Sometimes that means stepping out of your comfort zone. Other times it means showing restraint from what your logic tells you to do. Sometimes God instructed David to advance into battle; other times He instructed him to wait. Faith doesn't wear one shoe size. Nor does it look the same in each situation. To live with kingdom faith as a kingdom hero means you choose to stay so close to God that pleasing Him becomes your highest concern. Honoring Him becomes the way you roll. Pursuing Him and His ways becomes your normal flow. When you learn to do that, you'll be amazed at what God will do for you.

Know the Value of Your Walk

A man once robbed a bank in Ottawa, Canada, stealing $6,000. But the interesting part of the story is this: When they arrested him and took him to jail, they discovered he'd used a 1918 semiautomatic colt revolver to commit that crime. Now, anyone who knows anything about guns already understands the point of this story. This gun was valued at more than $100,000, yet this man robbed a bank for only $6,000. He could have simply sold the gun and walked away with more than ten times what he got in the robbery. But he didn't sell the gun because he didn't know the worth of what he held in his hand.

This bank robber thought what he had was only good for threatening people. He thought it only allowed him to force his way into a situation under his direct control. If he'd only known that what he had was worth far more than his human attempt to gain something on his own, he never would have been locked up for thievery. He would have sold the gun rather than use it to rob a bank.

Similarly, if you ever discover all that you have in your relationship with God and your faith walk with Him, like Sarah did after nearly 25 years of learning through mistakes, you'll understand that you don't have to settle for cheap substitutes. You don't have to spend your time stuck in a prison of bitterness, resentment, regret, hopelessness, or blame. Rather, if you just look at the value of what you already have in God by faith and how it can be used to bring about a greater good and God's glory, then you, too, will experience the fullness of His promises made manifest in your life. You, too, will laugh with a heart full of happiness and peace.

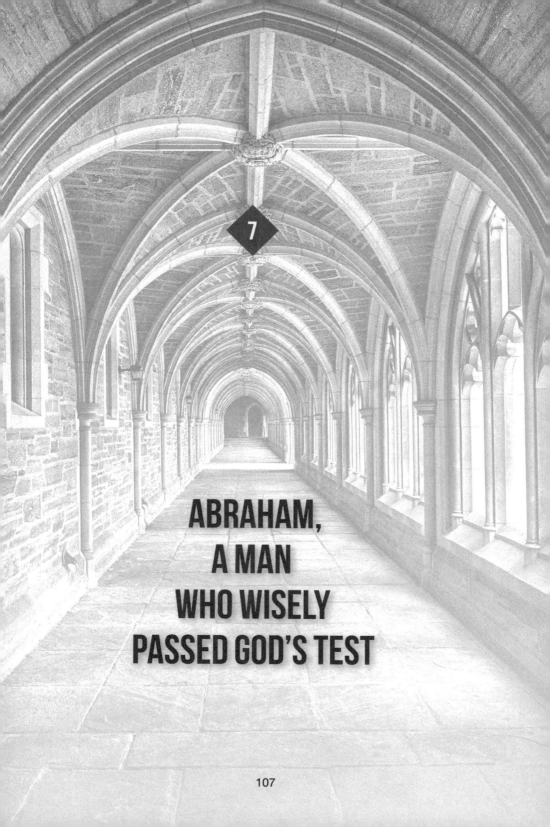

7

ABRAHAM, A MAN WHO WISELY PASSED GOD'S TEST

School, by its nature, includes tests. When it comes time to evaluate what a student has learned, the teacher delivers a test in order to gauge intellectual growth. The results of the test reveal if the student really knows the information given.

Some tests come as a surprise. We call them pop quizzes. These involve shorter exams given at a previously unannounced time. The idea is to make sure students remain vigilant, always ready for the unexpected test.

Then beyond pop quizzes, we have the more involved and official tests. Some of these are midterms. Others are finals. Finals often carry more weight than midterms because they're more extensive. They seek to cover a lot of ground in a short amount of time. Passing them means you can move on to the next grade level or year. Failing them means you're stuck where you are, and to go on, you have to learn the information all over again.

You can expect a test when God is ready to give you a new level of experience with Him and take you to a new level of your personal expression as a kingdom hero, advancing His cause on earth. You don't get to move forward just because you want to. First, you need to demonstrate that you're able to move forward.

The bad news is that a test is just that—a test. But the good news is that a test is preparation for a higher level, so that means you have something great to look forward to on the other side.

Some tests seem to stretch on forever. Rather than sitting down to one final exam, you experience the compounding effect of multiple tests back-to-back. At times, this can feel even more difficult than taking one major exam. But whatever the case, whether tests come as pop quizzes, midterms, finals, or a series of smaller tests, each one stacked on the last, God uses these tests to determine whether we're ready for the next stage of our journey.

We already looked at Abraham in the Hall of Heroes when we examined his willingness to leave his comfort zone and the known security that comes from a shared history in a place. After that, we entered the exhibit for Sarah and Abraham together. This took us through several Bible stories and accounts. Now, as we move on through the Hall of Heroes, we'll continue to look at the life of Abraham.

By now he has his son of the promise, and we see a sculpture of him and Isaac working together in a field. They look happy. Content. Off to the side, we read the next part of the narrative, which teaches us important lessons on faith. Inscribed on a placard beside Abraham and his son are these words:

> By faith Abraham, when he was tested, offered up Isaac, and he who had received the promises was offering up his only begotten son; it was he to whom it was said, "In Isaac your descendants shall be called." He considered that God is able to raise people even from the dead, from which he also received him back as a type (Hebrews 11:17-19).

The smiles we see on their two faces will soon disappear in the middle of the upcoming test. It will be a difficult test for them both. Greater details are recorded for us in Genesis 22, where we learn that Abraham has been told to offer up Isaac, the one through whom the promise of his heritage would be fulfilled, as a sacrifice. This isn't a pop quiz; this is a major test. You'll know when a test is major because it will call for something significant in your life to be addressed while you're simultaneously asked to address it in a way that makes no sense. When God is asking you to do something or be something or go somewhere you've never even considered, it's a major exam. It wasn't on your bucket list. In fact, it seems downright ridiculous.

Now, so you won't think I'm exaggerating the extent of Abraham's test, let's take a look at the exact words God spoke when He set the test before him. A large Bible sits on a stand in front of us as we walk past the display with Abraham and Isaac in the field. It's opened to Genesis 22, and these words have been highlighted for us:

> It came about after these things, that God tested Abraham, and said to him, "Abraham!" And he said, "Here I am." He said, "Take now your son, your only son, whom you love, Isaac, and go to the land of Moriah, and offer him there as a burnt offering on one of the mountains of which I will tell you" (verses 1-2).

A Clear Test—with Contradictions

God didn't mince His words in calling Abraham to the table for this test. He even acknowledged that the son He was asking him to sacrifice was the son he loved. What's more, he described the type of offering he wanted— a burnt offering. There was no lack of clarity here.

But this test did have a plethora of contradictions. As we move through the remainder of this exhibit on Abraham, we'll see five of them, each identified on a numbered sign, and we'll take a brief look at each one before moving on to the test itself. Doing so will help us better identify those times in our lives when God is asking us to step out in faith despite what makes sense.

1. The Theological Contradiction

For starters, the test involved a theological contradiction. God had made a promise to birth an entire nation through Isaac, but now He was telling Abraham to kill him. Isaac is still a teenager. He hasn't even married yet. He has no children of his own. If Abraham were to kill Isaac as God asked, he would be going against the very fulfillment of the initial promise itself. Logic could never figure that out because it defies logic. Establishing a lineage through someone you're asked to remove from this earth isn't humanly possible.

2. The Biblical Contradiction

Second, the test included a biblical contradiction, because in Genesis 9, God condemns murder. God had made it completely clear that no person is to take the life of another person, yet here was God asking Abraham to take the life of his son. Thus, God not only contradicted His promise theologically but contradicted His commands canonically.

3. The Emotional Contradiction

As if that weren't enough, a third contradiction shows up—an emotional contradiction. We see this because God asks Abraham to kill the son he loves. This is the son he's waited decades for. Isaac is his pride, joy, and daily delight. We saw the smiles on their faces when we first entered this exhibit. Abraham spends nearly every waking moment with Isaac—teaching him, enjoying him, and raising him to be the future of a promised nation. Isaac is a moment-by-moment reminder of God's mercies and grace to Abraham, and yet God is asking him to override his own emotions of love, preservation, and devotion in order to kill him. None of this could have made any sense to Abraham.

4. The Relational Contradiction

Abraham was married to Sarah, and this was her son of promise as well. Abraham loved Sarah, and as her husband, his role was to provide for her and protect her. To slay their son could never be explained to her in a way she could accept or understand. In fact, that's probably why in Genesis 22:3 we read that Abraham got up early to go to the mountain. He wanted to hit the road quickly so Sarah wouldn't catch any idea of what was going on. If she had, she surely would have tried to put a stop to it before he even set off.

But the fifth contradiction, worse than all of the others, stands out the most.

5. *The Spiritual Contradiction*

In sacrificing Isaac, the son Abraham loved, God asked Abraham to worship Him.

Now, if ever there was a day you wouldn't feel like going to church, it would be the day your son died—especially if he died at your own hand. How would you worship God with a broken heart? How would you lift up God's name to be glorified when your heart is confused? How would you praise the Lord when He has thoroughly disappointed and failed you?

Most people wouldn't feel like worshipping God on a day like that. But God didn't indicate He cared how Abraham felt about it. He just instructed him to do it. Abraham was told to worship God during his most difficult moment in time.

But despite all of the contradictions inherent in the command to go and sacrifice his son, Abraham went. He obeyed God even though he didn't know how this thing would play out. God hadn't given him details. He'd only told him to go, and that when he got there, He would show him what to do next.

One of the reasons we don't get to see more details from God up front is that He's asking us to move without them. Remember, the true level of our faith is determined by our feet, not our feelings. It's found in what we do, not just in what we say. Once again, if there is no movement, there is no faith.

By now, Abraham had faith in his life. Because of that, he got up. He went. He moved toward the direction God told him to go even though it didn't make sense. Also, he never thought God would truly let his son die—or he believed if Isaac did die, God would raise him from the dead. We know this because of what he told the men who had come along to carry the wood and supplies, and we get to see what he tells them in the next part of this exhibit.

There, we notice that the floor beneath us feels like a mountainside. It's become rugged. Off to the side are statues of two men carrying wood and supplies. A sculpture of Abraham stands off to the side, looking like he's saying something, and over the loudspeaker, you hear these words:

> Stay here with the donkey, and I and the lad will go over there; and we will worship and return to you (Genesis 22:5).

Behind Abraham is his son. The look of confusion on Isaac's face is starting to become all the more apparent. The same look is mirrored by the men carrying the supplies. Yet Abraham shows only a small amount of concern. He still stands with a mark of confidence. And despite God telling him He wanted him to sacrifice Isaac as a burnt offering, Abraham tells the men that both he and Isaac will return after they worship. Abraham displayed a kingdom hero move right then because he chose to speak out in faith.

Far too many people choose to speak words that confirm a negative reality rather than speak the truth in the midst of contradictions. Abraham knew the truth. He knew Isaac was the son of promise through whom God would establish an entire nation. And as we saw in Hebrews 11, Abraham knew death was no match for God. In fact, God could raise the dead just as easily as He could create life within a deadened womb. Abraham was certain that if he obeyed God and did what He asked him to do, all the while never wavering in belief on the promise given to him, then God would make all things work out. He was no longer afraid.

The apostle Paul confirmed this when he wrote,

> In hope against hope [Abraham] believed, so that he might become a father of many nations according to that which had been spoken, "So shall your descendants be." Without becoming weak in faith he contemplated his own body, now as good as dead since he was about a hundred years old, and the deadness of Sarah's womb; yet, with respect to the promise of God, he did not waver in unbelief but grew strong in faith, giving glory to God, and being fully assured that what God had promised, He

was able also to perform. Therefore it was also credited to him as righteousness (Romans 4:18-22).

Abraham hadn't forgotten the power of God showing up in his life throughout his history. That's why he had such confidence that God could handle an even bigger challenge in his present reality. He'd finally made it to the point of passing yesterday's exams, and he was determined to apply those lessons in the current test. Abraham had learned that failing an exam only meant having to relearn the wisdom necessary in order to take it again. He'd learned to trust God despite how things appeared.

Isaac, on the other hand, got nervous—and understandably so. After all, he and his dad set off to the altar to worship God with everything they needed except the sacrifice itself. But whatever thoughts were racing through Isaac's mind, they didn't take too long to come out of his mouth in a question. "My father!...Behold, the fire and the wood, but where is the lamb for the burnt offering?" (Genesis 22:7).

Abraham wasn't rattled by Isaac's question. Rather, he set out to put his son at ease with his reply. We hear verse 8 over the loudspeaker, again in the voice of Abraham: "God will provide for Himself the lamb for the burnt offering, my son." Essentially, he acknowledged to Isaac that he didn't have a solid answer for him right then, but he also assured him that God would fix it and it would all work out in the end.

Abraham's words had calmed Isaac enough to keep going, and now we hear their footsteps echoing beside us as we continue through the exhibit. When their footsteps stop, we've arrived at a large replica of the altar father and son built together. And on the altar lies Isaac.

When God Asks for Sacrifice

Now, Isaac lived in a day when and a culture where child sacrifice took place. He'd heard the horror stories about false religions and idol worship. So when he found himself on the altar, maybe he thought his dad was getting a little too old after all. Could Alzheimer's have set in and his dad had forgotten that they served the one, true God who condemned child sacrifice even though the false religions all around them did not? None of us would have blamed Isaac if he said, "Have you lost your mind? What's going on here, Dad?"

But off to the side of our altar replica is a bright light shining, out of which we hear these words from the angel of the Lord, calling from heaven:

> Do not stretch out your hand against the lad, and do nothing to him; for now I know that you fear God, since you have not withheld your son, your only son, from Me (verse 12).

The test was done. Abraham had passed, and Isaac could breathe a sigh of relief. But even though the test is done, something has caught my attention in what the angel said— "now I know." Did you hear that? The angel was speaking for God, but God is omniscient. And omniscient means all-knowing. God isn't confined by time or limited by a finite understanding. He sits outside of time and knows all that has taken place and will take place. So why does God send a message to Abraham saying "now I know"? That makes about as much sense as His original command to sacrifice his son. That is, until we look more closely at what it means to "know."

You see, just because God knows everything informationally and potentially doesn't mean He knows everything experientially. For example, if you were to ask God what it feels like to commit a sin, He couldn't answer that question because He's never committed a sin. God knows what sin is. He knows what sin produces. And He knows what it feels like to be sinned against. In fact, He can even tell you what it feels like to die for your sin, because, through Jesus Christ, He's experienced that. But God can't tell you what it feels like to commit a sin Himself because that's not a part of His experience (James 1:13).

Thus, while God knows everything, He hasn't experienced everything He knows. And that's why He became a man in the person of Jesus Christ— to be able to sympathize with our weaknesses. He wanted to feel what we were going through (Hebrews 4:5). God knows what we go through as human beings because Jesus has experienced what it feels like to be a human being.

In Abraham's situation, God knew Abraham loved Him. He'd heard Abraham tell Him that he loved Him. But God wanted more. He wanted a love He could feel. He wanted to experience the loving feelings associated with an intimacy built on trust. In order to do that, He asked Abraham to sacrifice the son whom he loved as a way of demonstrating that his greatest love was for God Himself.

God will often ask us to sacrifice what means the most to us as a way of demonstrating the level of our love for Him. It could be a person. It might be a dream, an ambition, a hope, a home, a business, material items, a relationship, a form of entertainment, our physical well-being, or anything else. Whatever exists in our lives as an "Isaac"—whatever we love the most—is often what God targets in our tests. This is because it's easy to let go of something that doesn't mean much or anything to us. Anyone can get rid of their trash, but not everyone can release what means the most to them.

But who ever said tests in the Kingdom Hero Academy would be easy? To live as a kingdom hero, you have to get through the grid of personal control and ownership in order to break through to the expansive space of God's preferred and creative will for your life.

Abraham hadn't counted on an intervention. Nor had he counted on a substitution. Scripture tells us he thought God would raise Isaac from the dead if he followed through and killed him. But Abraham wasn't about to argue with the method God chose to spare his son. He heard a ram caught in the thicket, then retrieved it and offered it as a substitute sacrifice to God. When he did, he chose to name the place "Jehovah-Jireh," which means "the Lord will provide." Just as Abraham had assured Isaac He would as they walked toward the altar empty-handed, God provided all they needed to obey Him completely.

By the way, the name Jireh means "to see beforehand." When you combine it with the name Jehovah, God's covenantal name, it more literally translates into "God's provision is tied to His prevision." God comes through for you when He's seen that you will remain faithful to Him. That's why all the while Abraham was walking up one side of the mountain, a ram was walking up the other. God "pre-saw" what Abraham would do, so He provided what Abraham would need.

The ram was in the vicinity of the sacrifice the whole time. But God kept it quiet until it was time for Abraham to know it was there, until Abraham had demonstrated a heroic level of faith. Here's what we discover from Abraham's experience of God's provision only after he exhibited actions reflecting a heart full of faith: We may not always see the solution prior to our commitment to the sacrifice.

Abraham didn't get the ram just because he walked up the mountain. He wasn't shown the ram when he set out toward the altar. He didn't even get the ram when he placed the wood in a stack in order to light it. The provision was provided when Abraham's faith reached the culmination of demonstrating the entirety of commitment God requires. His solution was revealed only when the knife was about to come down. It wasn't until Abraham completed his act of obedience that God's *pre*vision became *pro*vision for him.

Whatever God is seeking to do in your life and circumstances, He has already *pre*-seen. He's been there and back again. In Isaiah 46:10, He puts it like this: "Declaring the end from the beginning, and from ancient times things which have not been done, saying, 'My purpose will be established, and I will accomplish all My good pleasure.'"

But you won't get to see God's provision until you've completed what He's asked you to do. See, most Christians are part-time saints. They'll do a little something for God here or there when it's convenient, but few are willing to truly sacrifice their own wants, desires, comfort, and needs to advance His kingdom and promote His glory. The problems arise when part-time saints look to God for full-time blessing. It doesn't work that way.

Have you ever asked your kids to clean their rooms only to have them clean up halfway and expect a reward? They want you to congratulate them for doing half of the work you asked them to do. No parent in their right mind would just pat their kid on the back and say, "Well done. You did it!"

What parents say to their kids in that kind of situation—and without thinking twice about it—is what God often says to us: *Finish what I've asked you to do.* We aren't called to be part-time kingdom heroes. There's no such thing as a part-time hero anyway. What would happen if Batman chose to answer the Batphone only when he felt like it? He would quickly be relegated from hero status to punk. Part-time doesn't cut it when dealing with life-or-death situations.

Abraham knew that. He'd learned that lesson the hard way. But now he'd reached the point in his life when he could finally pass a test of this magnitude. And pass it he did. In fact, James 2:21-24 tells us Abraham not only passed the test with flying colors but got promoted to a unique level—a friend of God.

> Was not Abraham our father justified by works when he offered up Isaac his son on the altar? You see that faith was working with his works, and as a result of the works, faith was perfected; and the Scripture was fulfilled which says, "And Abraham believed God, and it was reckoned to him as righteousness," and he was called the friend of God.

Granted, God loves everyone. Each of us is loved by God. But not everyone is known as God's friend. A friend is a special status. Jesus described it like this: "You are My friends if you do what I command you" (John 15:14). Abraham became known as God's friend because he was willing to believe God against the backdrop of the ridiculous.

If you've never seen God move against the backdrop of the ridiculous or taken part in a final exam that made no utter sense at all, you've not truly seen what faith can produce. You're still operating by sight. You see only what you see. And if all you see is what you see, you won't see all there is to be seen. As a result, you'll forfeit the rewards of faith, which include the blessing and favor of God on your life.

An Oath and a Type

Abraham got the rewards of living as a kingdom hero. He got it all, because he was willing to offer it all, first and foremost, to God—in faith. Genesis 22:15-18 describes his rewards and how they are tied to his living and active faith.

> Then the angel of the LORD called to Abraham a second time from heaven, and said, "By Myself I have sworn, declares the LORD, because you have done this thing and have not withheld your son, your only son, indeed I will greatly bless you, and I will greatly multiply your seed as the stars of the heavens and as the sand which is on the seashore; and your seed shall possess the gate of their enemies. In your seed all the nations of the earth shall be blessed, because you have obeyed My voice."

God first gave this promise to bless Abraham when Abraham was around 75 years old. But then it was just a promise. Following Abraham's heroic step of faith, God declared that this promise had now become an oath. He said, "By Myself I have sworn…"

An oath is where God repeats a promise He's made in the past and attaches a time to its fulfillment. An oath ushers in the fulfillment of a promise. Once Abraham passed the final exam, God's promise became an oath even though Abraham had failed in the past. And even though Abraham had delayed the promise through his own wrong choices, God still brought it about. Abraham had grown to the point where he could pass the test of faith necessary for God to usher in the tangible reality of the promise given to him (Hebrews 6:13-18).

When Scripture says Abraham received Isaac back as "a type," it reveals God's ability to meet us in our trials and use them to take us to a new spiritual level with Him. Some of you may have been taking the same test over and over and over. You feel like life is one continuous retest of the same test you keep failing. You feel trapped in a loop. Perhaps that's caused you to focus on your failures or your mistakes.

But rather than focus on the times you haven't passed, I want you to focus on the fact that God always allows a retest. You can choose to make the next right decision even when your past decisions have been less than great. It all starts now. What God did for Abraham is a picture of what He can do for you.

Focus on Jesus

On this journey of faith, if you're struggling because God is asking you to release something you want to hold on to more tightly than anything else, remember Abraham's story. Stand and stare at his bust in the Hall of Heroes for a moment. Remember what he went through in order to make it in there. What's more, remember what Abraham saw in faith, because you have the ability to see it too—if you will open your heart and your eyes.

As we read earlier, Abraham looked up and saw the place of sacrifice when he was climbing the mountain (Genesis 22:4). In John 8, Jesus gives us greater detail into what Abraham actually saw. He's explaining to the Pharisees that He is the Son of God, and they're questioning Him on how this could be true. Jesus tells them, "Your father Abraham rejoiced to see My day, and he saw it and was glad" (John 8:56).

On his way to Mount Moriah to sacrifice his son, Abraham saw more than just a location in the distance. He saw God's plan. Mount Moriah is only a few hundred yards from Calvary. Not much land separates the two. So as Abraham walked toward the location of his sacrifice, he got a glimpse into the greatest Sacrifice of all. And it made him glad. He smiled. Deep within him, he knew all he needed to know: The Lord will provide.

That's why Hebrews 12:2 reminds all kingdom heroes in training that where they choose to focus matters. It says "fixing our eyes on Jesus, the author and perfecter of faith." While you journey, look to Jesus. While you climb, look to Christ. While you face life's tests, look to the face of the One who knows just how this thing will end. Keep your eyes on Jesus. He will sustain your faith until you reach the final question on your exam.

Abraham passed one of the most difficult tests that could ever be given to a person. He did so because he chose to look at the greatest Hero of all time. He chose to keep his eyes and his heart locked on the unfailing love and provision of Jesus Christ.

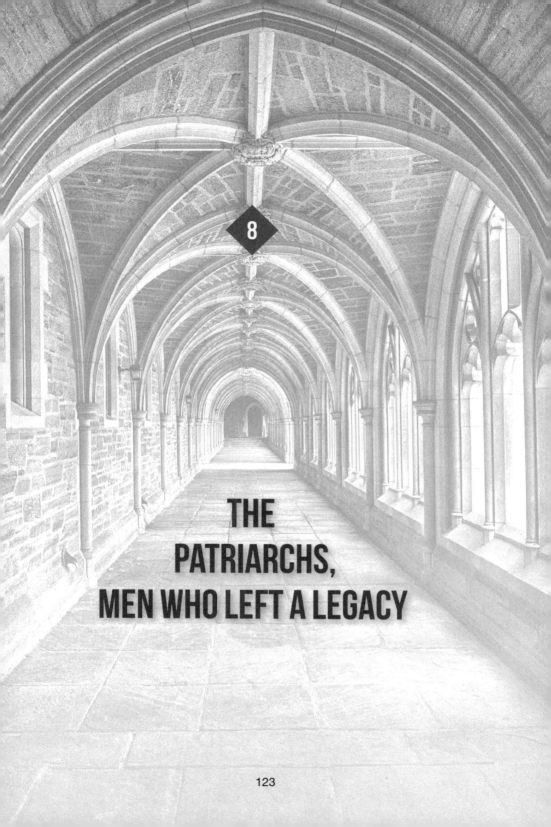

8

THE
PATRIARCHS,
MEN WHO LEFT A LEGACY

When the kids were young, we took them to Disneyland. They loved to watch Mickey Mouse, Minnie Mouse, and especially Goofy on television, and we thought it would be a nice experience for them to meet those characters "in person." It was a long drive from Texas to California, but we finally made it to the Magic Kingdom.

We were there during the peak of vacation season, so the place was packed. And after a while, Lois and I got so caught up in all of the fun and excitement that—I'll admit it—we let down our guard. We weren't paying attention to the kids as closely as we had when we first got there. And before we knew it, our youngest son, Jonathan, was no longer with us.

Little Jon-Jon, as we called him then (and still do on occasion today), had wandered off when we weren't watching. We immediately started looking in the vicinity where we were, but he was nowhere to be seen. We then spanned out and searched in different directions, but we still couldn't find him. As panic rose in our hearts, making time nearly stand still in our minds, I went to a security station to report our son was missing. The security staff set out looking as well, scanning the park for any signs of him.

In a place where there should have been nothing but joy, fun, and festivities, we found ourselves despondent and scared. The so-called Magic Kingdom hadn't turned out to be that magical after all. It took some time before we found Jonathan, but we eventually located him in a toy store looking at all the displays. Grateful to have found him, we'd also become weary by the scare and search, thus dampening our enthusiasm for the remainder of the day.

We faced a dual problem that day in Disneyland. First, Jonathan had become distracted by the sights and sounds of the kingdom he was in. Second, *we'd* become distracted by the sights and sounds of the kingdom we were in. We'd all become distracted by the imagery, music, rides, and thrills in the Magic Kingdom. In fact, we'd become so focused on that kingdom that we lost our focus on what mattered most—our son. In other words, being in that very kingdom had resulted in us, as parents, losing contact with our own child.

Today, you and I are living in a world where, if we don't intently focus on God's kingdom, we can easily be pulled away into the lure of another kingdom. The competing kingdom of darkness to God's kingdom of light would like nothing more than to woo both us and our families into a scenario of chaos, separation, and despair. Yes, it will use the illusion of excitement and fun to get us there, but once sucked in, we'll discover it was all smoke and mirrors.

While our study on how to live life as a kingdom hero isn't on parenting, we can glean certain key principles concerning parenting—and mentoring and leading—from our next exhibit in the Hall of Heroes. Keep in mind, you don't need to be a parent to influence the next generation or leave a legacy. Many families have aunts, uncles, or even friends who choose to invest in the raising of their children in such a meaningful way that the impact is nearly the same as the parent's, if not in some cases even more. The nature of the parent and child relationship, whether biological or through adoption, matters less than the nature of the relationship connectedly.

In Hebrews 11:20-22, we discover a key outcome when we choose to live as kingdom heroes: our impact. Some people call it your legacy. Others refer to it as your influence. Whatever term you want to give it isn't as important as recognizing the opportunity you have to leave a positive imprint on those around you. That's what kingdom heroes do. They influence and affect those around them for God's glory and others' good. Hebrews 11:20-22 tells us this is what happened with a group of people in Israel's earliest history.

We're introduced to this passage as we walk into the exhibit displaying three elderly Israelite men—Isaac, Jacob, and Joseph—along with their sons, grandsons, and other descendants. The three men are all animatronic with movements and gestures that reflect the Scripture written for us on a large plaque just to the right of the display.

> By faith Isaac blessed Jacob and Esau, even regarding things to come. By faith Jacob, as he was dying, blessed each of the sons of Joseph, and worshiped, leaning on the top of his staff. By faith Joseph, when he was dying, made mention of the exodus of the sons of Israel, and gave orders concerning his bones.

These men, along with Abraham, are the patriarchs. They're the fathers of Israel's faith. As such, they passed down a legacy of leadership to those who came after them. Of course, as we all know, patriarchs aren't the people who leave a lasting impact. As the saying goes, "The hand who rocks the cradle rules the world." The Hall of Heroes will introduce us to a woman who had equal impact through her role in raising up a future leader of Israel. But because of the order the heroes are mentioned in Hebrews, we'll first look at these three men who influenced Israel according to God's plan.

Isaac, Jacob, and Joseph passed on a blessing and a hope to those who came after them. Isaac blessed Jacob and Esau. Jacob blessed the sons of Joseph. And Joseph's faith was so strong that he imparted the belief of a brighter tomorrow by a command concerning his own burial location.

The best way I know to illustrate what leaving a spiritual legacy is in contemporary terms is to compare it to a legal document—a will. Everyone ought to have a will, especially if they have a family. It's irresponsible not to have one. A will controls what happens to all that God has blessed us with over the course of our life. It is a physical legacy concerning present personal and financial assets. We make a will so we—not someone else—choose what happens to what we'll leave behind when it's our time to transition to Glory.

You don't want someone else determining what happens to what you've worked so hard to obtain. You don't want family members or the courts fighting over the transfer of your assets. A will creates an orderly transference of what has been deposited in your care as a kingdom steward so it can be turned over for the well-being of and safe use by your family, offspring, or any other entity you choose to bless.

What we do with a will physically is what God expects each of us to do spiritually with a kingdom influence over those with whom we journey during our time on earth. Whether your will includes your family, coworkers, church members, friends, or a group or organization is entirely up to you, but as kingdom disciples, we're called to replicate the DNA of discipleship through us to others. This is done through an intentional pursuit of influence.

What we're witnessing in the devolution of our culture today is a lack of transference of kingdom values. We have a generation of individuals without a spiritual covering through God's covenant rising to positions of power and influence—and it's showing up in every facet of life. This is because God's kingdom followers have failed to emphasize the critical nature of a spiritual covering through the covenant.

One of the reasons the transfer hasn't occurred is that, to transfer something, you have to first own it. Yet we've slowly drifted away from a Christian culture set on studying the Word of God and applying it in our lives, instead drifting steadily toward a culture of spiritual snippets and short platitudes. If you have little faith, then you have few spiritual assets to pass on. If you have no faith, then you have no spiritual assets to pass on. As a result, our culture continues to rain down evil through the torrential cascade of secularism, commercialism, immorality, narcissism, and redefinitions of what God has established as His standards.

To live by a kingdom standard, you have to know what the kingdom standard is. Again, that's where so much of our society has gone wrong. We've moved too far away from God's Word. God knew the dangers of doing so, which is why He gave us instructions on how to stay close to Him in Deuteronomy 6:4-9. We read this passage as we look to the wall directly behind the three men and their families. It's written in large letters that cover the entirety of the wall, and in it, God lays out the blueprint for how we are to both identify with His standards and pass them on to others.

> Hear, O Israel! The LORD is our God, the LORD is one! You shall love the LORD your God with all your heart and with all your soul and with all your might. These words, which I am commanding you today, shall be on your heart. You shall teach them diligently to your sons and shall talk of them when you sit in your house and when you walk by the way and when you lie down and when you rise up. You shall bind them as a sign on your hand and they shall be as frontals on your forehead. You shall write them on the doorposts of your house and on your gates.

God gave clear instructions on how to transfer the values of His kingdom as well as how to raise a future generation of kingdom heroes. They involved the regular, ongoing exposure to and rehearsing of His Word. His truth was to be taught "diligently," a routine part of everyday life whether people were walking, sitting, coming in, or going out. There was to be no place anyone in the Israelite community could go without being exposed to God's Word.

Now, if we can no longer so much as have the Ten Commandments displayed in public places, it's no wonder our culture has taken a nosedive into the abyss of spiritual anarchy. When you remove God from the equation, you remove all that He brings with Him—such as peace, order, favor, and equity.

Leaving a spiritual legacy to those who come after you requires an intentional practice of impartation. It doesn't require being perfect. It requires that you are intentional. Neither Isaac nor Jacob would have been heralded as the "Father of the Year" by any committee.

Let's look at each of them.

Isaac

Isaac inherited his father's lying genes and inevitably lied about his own wife, Rebekah, at one point saying she was his sister. (Remember when Abraham told the same lie about Sarah?) Not only that, but the Bible lets us know he lied because he was afraid and selfish:

> When the men of the place asked about his wife, he said, "She is my sister," for he was afraid to say, "my wife," *thinking*, "the men of the place might kill me on account of Rebekah, for she is beautiful" (Genesis 26:7).

Whatever had been wrong in the gene pool, Isaac got a full dose of it.

Not only that, but Isaac was so absorbed by his own heart's leaning and his own desire for good food that he wanted to give the birthright blessing to the wrong person. God had chosen Jacob for Isaac to give the blessing to. But Isaac loved Esau more than Jacob, so he wanted to give it to Esau even though God instructed him differently. We read, "Now Isaac loved Esau, because he had a taste for game, but Rebekah loved Jacob" (Genesis 25:28). God had to allow a trick to be played on Isaac by both Rebekah and Jacob in order for the blessing of primary inheritance to get where God wanted it to go.

Jacob

Then, there's Jacob. Jacob had 12 children by four different women. He was a player knee-deep in baby-mama drama! Beyond that, he's known for being a deceiver, manipulator, and overall bad father. He literally raised up terrorists, rapists, and incestuous sons. He also raised up sons who would sell their younger brother, Joseph—Jacob's favorite son—into slavery. Jacob was messed up.

Thus, when we walk by the portrayals of Isaac and Jacob in the Hall of Heroes, we aren't walking by men who lived pristine lives and led their entire families and communities into great revivals by their example. We're walking by very human men who made significant mistakes early in life.

Yet they stand displayed in this hall because, despite their failures, they chose to have faith in God toward the latter part of their lives.

We see Jacob leaning on his staff and blessing his grandsons. He's leaning on his staff because he's old. But he's also leaning on it because he wrestled with the angel of the Lord many years earlier and got his heart set in alignment under God's rule (Genesis 32:22-32).

Isaac's and Jacob's placement in the Hall of Heroes ought to be good news for someone. It tells us God is the God of second chances. Or third chances. Or however many chances it takes to get right with Him. He can give you the chance to make up for the failures in your past if you'll apply what you've learned from those failures. You just need to grow. And as you grow, seek to bless those in your present with His kingdom influence through what you've learned.

You can't go back and change your past. No one can. But you have every opportunity to create a better tomorrow whenever you choose to do so.

Joseph

As a result of Jacob's return to God and surrender under His rule, his son Joseph was positioned to live out a strong life of faith on behalf of the Israelite people in Egypt. Joseph modeled his faith in many ways, one of which was his willingness to forgive his brothers for their egregious sin against him—selling him into slavery. His forgiveness came in a heart rooted in the belief that God is inherently good. As he said to his brothers in Genesis 50:20, "As for you, you meant evil against me, but God meant it for good in order to bring about this present result, to preserve many people alive." Joseph was able to forgive because he saw the hand of God in the troubles other people brought his way.

Joseph also spared his family from starvation, along with all of the Israelites, through his ability to live as a true disciple of God in the midst of a pagan land. His interpretation of Pharaoh's dreams led to the stockpiling of food for the ultimate worldwide famine, and his wisdom and leadership skills enabled him to integrate into another culture and rise to a position of great national influence.

By the time Joseph neared the end of his life, he was known as nothing less than a kingdom hero in the hearts and minds of his fellow Israelites. That's why when he demonstrated faith in asking them to carry his bones into the promised land, the people agreed to do it.

Pass the Baton of Faith

Most of us have witnessed the excitement of a relay race, seeing men and women run as fast as they can to claim victory. However, as important as each runner's speed is, it's equally critical whether and how they pass the baton. No matter how fast the runners are, if they fail to successfully pass the baton, their efforts will have been in vain. Relay races are about legacy, about transferring an essential tool to the next person on the journey to reach an agreed-upon destiny and goal.

God is a generational God, and His goal for us throughout history is to advance His kingdom agenda from one generation to the next (Daniel 4:3,34). This is why throughout Scripture, over and over again, He declares that He is the God of Abraham, Isaac, and Jacob (see Exodus 3:16; 4:5; 2 Chronicles 30:6). The baton He's given us to pass on is a living, active faith in Him based on His inerrant Word. When that faith is dropped or not transferred properly, not only is the proper expansion of His kingdom compromised but our lives, families, churches, and communities are void of the full experience of His power and His promises.

The good news, however, is that in His grace, God gives us new opportunities to pick up the baton of faith and keep going. God gave Jacob a new opportunity to pick up the baton he'd dropped due to his own sin through the blessing of his grandsons (Genesis 48:8-22) and the restoration of the broken relationship between his sons.

So if you've dropped the baton of living out your faith and transferring it to those in your sphere of influence, there's still hope. Rather than seeing you walk off the track of your life in defeat, God wants to restore you from the failures of yesterday to the victory of tomorrow. You can still cross the finish line of life as a winner.

This is why I love Jeremiah 29:11-14, where God promises His people who have failed spiritually that, if they will return to Him, He will still fulfill His plan for their lives and restore to them what they lost because of their sin.

When I was a boy growing up in Baltimore, I loved to go duckpin bowling at our local bowling alley. Duckpin bowling utilized small bowling balls, and because technology was crude back then, the machinery to reset the knocked-down pins didn't always work properly. That's why a man whose responsibility it was would go from lane to lane, manually resetting those pins. You never saw his face, just his feet.

If sin and circumstances have knocked you over, causing you to drop the baton of transferring a living faith to advance God's kingdom agenda to the next generation, I have great news for you. The invisible God is going from life to life, willing and ready to pick up the fallen pieces of yours and set them straight again so you can roll on to spiritual victory as a kingdom hero intent on leaving a kingdom legacy.

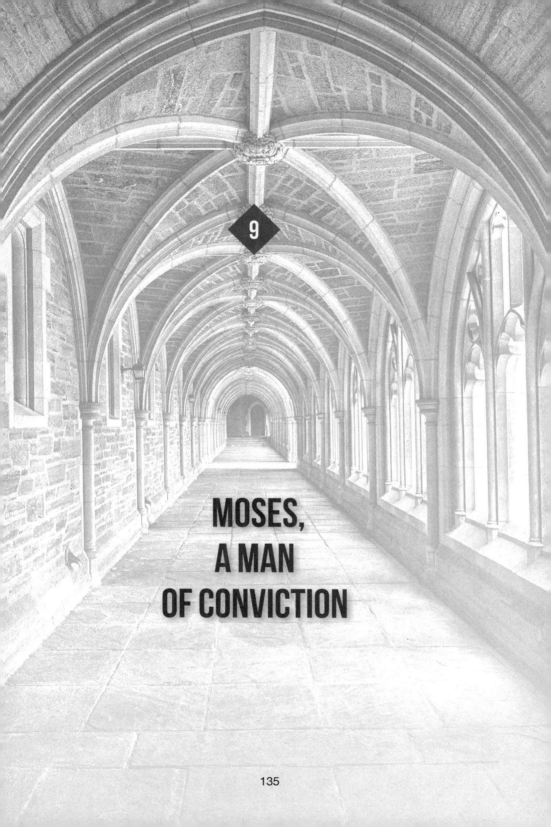

9

MOSES,
A MAN
OF CONVICTION

Having walked past the Hall of Heroes exhibit on Isaac, Jacob, and Joseph, we now enter into a long hallway with murals on both sides. The first images are of reeds, making it seem like we're near a river. We can smell the hint of fresh foliage nearby, causing us to feel as if we're walking in the region ourselves. Sounds of water rippling to the edges of the shore capture our attention. Just beyond one of the tall bunches of wild reeds, we see a young girl's face peeking through. She's looking into the river, where a tar-bottomed basket floats. Inside the basket sleeps the Israelites' hope for freedom.

You and I know him as Moses. And while you might think this entire section of the Hall of Heroes is dedicated to him, we first gain a glimpse into how he grew into the great man of God he would one day become. The words of Hebrews 11:23 are written on a plaque midway down the hallway:

> By faith Moses, when he was born, was hidden for three months by his parents, because they saw he was a beautiful child; and they were not afraid of the king's edict.

Not afraid. Those two words sum up how Moses grew to express such greatness. The parents who gave him life were "not afraid." They lived with faith over fear. The DNA passed down to their son through this genetic transfer was that of belief.

But even more than that, Moses' parents' lack of fear in the face of an evil culture and evil king spared his life. They chose to hide him so he would not be killed, as the king of Egypt had mandated midwives do away with male Hebrew babies as soon as they were born. Then, when Moses had grown too old to hide, they came up with an elaborate scheme to position him in a safe and secure place. Looking at their plan as a strategist, you might even say they sought to infiltrate the system that oppressed them through this act of faith, in order to bring about a positive influence for good. In a sense, Moses was a fifth columnist.

The strategy, as you probably know, involved placing Moses in a basket, in the Nile River near the place where Pharaoh's daughter bathed, accompanied by her maids. Knowing that he was a beautiful baby, they assumed the best of her feminine instincts. And they were right. With one look at this crying infant, she "had pity on him and said, 'This is one of the Hebrews' children'" (Exodus 2:6).

Now, Moses' parents knew Pharaoh's daughter would not be in a position to raise a child on her own. Those types of roles were for servants in that cultural time period. So they'd also placed Moses' sister, Miriam, where she could keep an eye on the basket and present herself when it was retrieved. That's who we see peeking through the reeds in our exhibit.

The plan went according to their hopes, and when Miriam offered to find someone to help nurse the boy and care for him in the palace, Pharaoh's daughter agreed. Miriam was more than willing to offer her mother to do just that.

As we near the end of the murals on the hallway walls, we see the baby being drawn from the basket, we hear the water dropping off the basket as it's lifted from the river, and from a loudspeaker, we hear the Bible passage that describes the rest of the scene:

> Pharaoh's daughter said to [Moses' mother], "Take this child away and nurse him for me and I will give you your wages." So the woman took the child and nursed him. The child grew, and she brought him to Pharaoh's daughter and he became her son.

> And she named him Moses, and said, "Because I drew him out
> of the water" (Exodus 2:5-10).

Not only was Moses' life spared from certain death in the violent culture he'd been born into, but his mother was paid to nurse him and raise him in the palace. This truth reminds us that we will never discover what God can do until we trust Him to do it. He can do things that blow our minds. Moses' parents had decided they would not be controlled by the culture, so their decisions reflected alignment under the one, true God.

Living by faith means choosing God's plan over the culture's plan, then watching Him work it out for your good and others' benefit.

Moses Makes a Decision of His Own

The impact made by Moses' mother raising him is prominent in the narrative as we exit the hallway and witness live actors on a screen portraying the next portions of Moses' life. They begin in Hebrews 11:24-25.

> By faith Moses, when he had grown up, refused to be called the
> son of Pharaoh's daughter, choosing rather to endure ill-treatment
> with the people of God than to enjoy the passing pleasures of sin.

How did Moses come to this conclusion? First, while his mother was nursing him and raising him in the palace, she used her proximity to him to shape his future worldview. She instilled in him a heart for his own people, seeking to solidify a connection with his authentic identity in his mind. Her influence made an impact as we see by Moses' decisions as an adult. His faith in what his mother taught him, which ultimately translated into faith in the one, true God, dictated his choices and shaped his values. As we see in the Scripture above, when (according to Acts 7:23) Moses was around 40, he refused to be called the son of Pharaoh's daughter any longer.

Keep in mind that this decision came at great personal cost. By that time Moses had wealth, women, power, comfort, and education. Yet despite all that, he made a choice to no longer be associated with the Egyptians. He was able to do this because of the impact his mother had on his life. Over the years she was allowed to raise him, she reminded him that he wasn't like the others. He'd been spared for a purpose and a calling on his life.

Moses had carefully considered his options. He didn't make an impulsive decision. Hebrews 11:26 tells us he chose what he did because he was "looking to the reward." He, like Abraham, looked ahead to see more than what could be seen in the present reality. Thus, his focus determined his future and the future of the entire nation of Israel. With his upbringing and the influence of his mother, Moses knew more about his future and God's plan for him than he would have known without them. We recognize this to be true by what is written in the book of Acts, which gives us the second reason Moses chose to identify not with the Egyptians but with the Hebrews.

> When he was approaching the age of forty, it entered his mind to visit his brethren, the sons of Israel. And when he saw one of them being treated unjustly, he defended him and took vengeance for the oppressed by striking down the Egyptian. And he supposed that his brethren understood that God was granting them deliverance through him, but they did not understand (Acts 7:23-25).

Again, Moses had everything a man could ever want. As we saw in the passage above, he declared his initial stand with the Hebrews right around the age of 40. Now, while 40 wasn't middle aged during Moses' time on earth, it was still indicative of a point of maturity in a man's life. From three months old to 40 years old, Moses had lived large. He had all the money he could spend. He was potentially a future leader of the leading country and culture at that time.

But despite all of this, he took a stand. He made a choice. He made a decision. He would no longer live with his feet planted only in midair. He said he no longer wanted to be viewed as the son of Pharaoh's daughter.

Moses knew God was going to grant the Israelites deliverance through him, but he didn't know this out of the clear blue sky. He knew because he'd been influenced to know while he was raised by his mother. And while Moses would make mistakes along the path of the Hebrews' deliverance, he did eventually arrive at the place God intended for him all along. This imperfect man learned what he needed through life's lessons, and he ultimately led God's chosen people to freedom.

For Such a Time as This

Moses' stand was somewhat clumsy, to say the least. He didn't necessarily think it through. But one thing was crystal clear: He took vengeance for his people by killing an Egyptian who mistreated a Hebrew worker. He crossed the red line. There was no explaining or turning back from an action like that. He made a choice, willing to live (or die) with the consequences.

Let me take a moment to use Moses as an example. I want to give you the whole truth here, and nothing but the truth. Once you make the clear choice to stand with God, you *will* experience ill treatment. You *will* suffer consequences. You *will* face fallout. So if you want to live your life as though you're in a popularity contest, the choice to follow God as His kingdom hero is not the choice for you. Obedience to God does not result in popularity with the world and contemporary culture. The apostle Paul said it as straightforward as it could possibly be said in his second letter to Timothy: "Indeed, all who desire to live godly in Christ Jesus will be persecuted" (2 Timothy 3:12).

Let that verse sink in. It doesn't say *some* people who choose to live godly in Christ Jesus will be persecuted. Neither does it say those who choose to live godly in Christ Jesus will face a *trouble here or there*. Rather, it says *everyone* who chooses to live godly in Christ Jesus will face *persecution*.

At the very least, negative repercussions will come your way if you make a stand for Jesus Christ. You may no longer be in the "in-crowd." You may no longer get the raises you've become accustomed to getting. You may be passed over for special recognition even though you deserve it. You may face opposition, bullying, or even public humiliation. That's why Hebrews 11:26 begins with an important phrase: "considering the reproach of Christ." To consider something means to think it through carefully. The whole verse says Moses considered "the reproach of Christ greater riches than the treasures of Egypt; for he was looking to the reward."

Just before this passage, in Hebrews 11:25, we read that Moses chose not to "enjoy the passing pleasures of sin." What this reminds us of is important. Sin is fun. Sin can be enjoyable. Anyone who tells you differently either hasn't sinned or is lying. Because if sin were as terrible as taking a spoonful of castor oil, no one would be tempted to take part in it. The reason sin is addictive is because it feels so good. Thus, the Bible is not trying to hide that reality.

But the second thing we discover in this passage is that while sin is fun, it's also a passing pleasure at best. That's why a person has to keep sinning to experience sin's highest level of enjoyment. In fact, sin often requires an even greater level of sin to provide the same pleasure. You have to up the dosage to get the same impact. This is what often turns sin into an addiction.

But rather than get caught up in the fleeting pleasures of sin, Moses made a decision for long-term gain. He made a cost-benefit analysis. He looked at the pros and cons. He chose to consider "the reproach of Christ" as "greater riches than the treasures of Egypt" (verse 26), and with that we see the why behind his decision. He knew if he sided with God and His people, he would be positioning himself for the greater reward up ahead. And Moses did not want to miss it.

The Reward

So many memories stand out from the season of my wife's passing after 49 years of marriage. I so often think of things Lois said, looks she gave, and special moments we shared during her last year of life on earth. But one thing in particular stands out to me right now as I'm thinking about Moses and his decision. It's something Lois said.

Just a few days before she was to transition to Glory, Lois was lying quietly in bed. Suddenly, her voice—which had previously been weak, making her speech difficult to understand at times—spoke loud and clear. "My award," she said with a smile coming across her face. "They are going to give me an award!" It's as if she could already see what lay ahead—the eternal reward for a lifetime of dedication and service to our great God and King.

That statement, among other things, brought me great comfort about Lois's homegoing. I knew there was a lot for her to enjoy there, and that she would be rewarded fully for her sacrifice and ministry on earth.

Moses knew the eternal award that awaited him in the hands of the one, true God would be much more meaningful than anything he might experience on this earth, no matter how fun it might be in the moment. He understood what truly mattered, which is why he made the choice he did. He picked a side.

But I don't think Moses was thinking only of an eternal reward. Again, we have to keep in mind that his mother's voice had been speaking to him since the time of his birth. She'd given him the history of the Hebrew people. She'd told him the stories of Abraham and the agreement he and God made—that one day there would be an entire nation. She shared with him the promise of a land and that someone would need to lead them there. We don't know for sure, but she probably told him he was the one to do so. After all, he'd been placed in the palace for such a time as this.

Moses' mother no doubt urged him not to settle for the junk of Egypt while missing out on the reward of God's promise for the Hebrew people. He was a leader. He was intelligent. He'd been spared and chosen by God Himself. I'm sure she didn't want her son to fall so in love with the world that he would miss out on God's plan for his life altogether, even though that's easy to do. People can fall so in love with secular society that they wind up dying with money in the bank, a big house, and a nice car but a wasted life because they never got around to experiencing God's plan for them.

The reward of God is greater than the treasures of man. But unless you believe that you won't make the wise decision like Moses did. You'll wind up hanging out with the world rather than giving yourself fully to God.

Moses made up his mind as a result of his faith in both a reward to experience in his lifetime and an eternal one. Hebrews 11:27 explains it like this: "By faith he left Egypt, not fearing the wrath of the king; for he endured, as seeing Him who is unseen." Moses exercised faith in choosing God's presence over the earthly king. Yet as I mentioned earlier, he didn't necessarily think it through. By jumping out there to kill the Egyptian before making any clear headway in his relationship with the Hebrew people, he left not much more than confusion on the table and a bad taste in the mouths of those he sought to help.

Through that graphic mistake, he wound up running for his life. His presumptive spirit led him on a detour that lasted for decades. While Moses assumed the Hebrews would know he was acting as their deliverer, he made the mistake of not checking with God first. He tried to do a good thing, but it ended up being a bad thing altogether.

Yet God, despite Moses' wrong action, knew his heart and motive had been right. That just didn't remove the consequence of his unwise choice.

The Calling

On a large electronic board, Moses' story continues with Acts 7:25-30 scrolling for visitors to read as they walk through the room.

> He supposed that his brethren understood that God was granting them deliverance through him, but they did not understand. On the following day he appeared to them as they were fighting together, and he tried to reconcile them in peace, saying, "Men, you are brethren, why do you injure one another?" But the one who was injuring his neighbor pushed him away, saying, "Who made you a ruler and judge over us? You do not mean to kill me as you killed the Egyptian yesterday, do you?" At this remark, Moses fled and became an alien in the land of Midian, where he became the father of two sons. After forty years had passed, an angel appeared to him in the wilderness of Mount Sinai, in the flame of a burning thorn bush.

Moses' impulsive decision led him to a four-decades-long detour herding sheep. This imperfect man, who somehow wound up in the Hall of

Heroes, had many lessons to learn over a long period of time. But God eventually did appear to him as he was shepherding his sheep in the wilderness area of Mount Sinai.

This is the scene we see as we walk even further through the hall. Off to the right side is a large bush. You can see it's burning yet not being consumed. Over to the left-hand side is another animatronic man, this one crouching in fear or timidity—you can't quite decide by looking at him. A loud voice sounds overhead: "Moses, Moses!"

Then you hear a faint voice coming from the direction of the crouching man. "Here I am," he says.

The same booming voice bursts forth again. "Do not come near here; remove your sandals from your feet, for the place on which you are standing is holy ground...I am the God of your father, the God of Abraham, the God of Isaac, and the God of Jacob" (Exodus 3:5-6).

After this, you notice the crouching man removes his shoes, after which he crouches even lower and seeks to hide his face. His fear and awe overwhelm him. But the commanding voice of God speaks once again.

> I have surely seen the affliction of My people who are in Egypt, and have given heed to their cry because of their taskmasters, for I am aware of their sufferings. So I have come down to deliver them from the power of the Egyptians, and to bring them up from that land to a good and spacious land, to a land flowing with milk and honey, to the place of the Canaanite and the Hittite and the Amorite and the Perizzite and the Hivite and the Jebusite. Now, behold, the cry of the sons of Israel has come to Me; furthermore, I have seen the oppression with which the Egyptians are oppressing them. Therefore, come now, and I will send you to Pharaoh, so that you may bring My people, the sons of Israel, out of Egypt (Exodus 3:7-10).

You know this as the calling of Moses. You recognize this as one of his heroic stories. What's more, you know how this story ends. The now fearful and timid Moses learns to trust God and His power to work both in him and through him to lead the Hebrew people to freedom.

I don't want to go into those details now because we'll cover them in the next chapter and the next section of the museum. But I do want to remind you that, based on Moses' life story, even though you may be shaky in your faith right now or timid in times of confusion and doubt, God can raise you up and strengthen you to complete great works for Him. You may identify with Moses in his impulsivity during his younger years. Or maybe with him in his insecurity in his older years. Whatever the case, Moses gives all of us an example of what it means to be redeemed from the frailties of our flesh and used by the power of God working in us. His story ought to inspire all of us to dream big as to what God can and will do through us for others.

There really is no end in sight if we commit ourselves to God's kingdom plan and seek to serve Him as kingdom heroes.

A good friend of mine is a successful business owner. Altogether, his various companies are valued in the billions. I always enjoy getting to spend time with him because his positive energy and enthusiasm light up any room he enters. He always has a new and bigger idea than the one he had the day before. He knows no fear. He moves forward with his visions and dreams in a unique way, pulling off what many can only hope for.

One reason he has been successful is that he understands the art and necessity of risk. He's spoken to me on several occasions about the "risk versus reward" factor in business. Oftentimes, the higher the risk in launching a new product, brand, or concept, the higher the potential reward. Sure, there's always some level of entrepreneurial risk involved with business start-ups or new lines of products, but frequently the riskiest of them all usher in the greatest success in return.

Now, granted, you can also stand to lose a lot when the risk is high, but savvy businesspeople understand that's just part of the equation of doing business with your sights set high.

The people we've seen in the Hall of Heroes all knew risk. They knew what it was like to put all of their eggs in God's basket. They went all-in, and because they did, they reaped an eternal and oftentimes also an earthly reward. Faith is risky business. But it comes with the opportunity to gain a tremendous reward if you put your faith in that which is worthy of it—God.

A risk involves taking a chance on something without any empirical evidence for where it will wind up. You can't prove whatever it is will turn out like you hope, but you still decide to move forward with the hope that it will.

Faith always involves risk, and God wants you to take a risk on Him because He knows He's dependable. The Bible tells us He is. So even though He's invisible to your eyes, you have His written Word. And God regularly makes promises He wants you to act on before you see them worked out. He creates opportunities for you to take a risk on what He's said. Oftentimes, He does that by allowing a spiritual crisis in your life to occur.

Now, when I say *spiritual crisis*, I'm not talking about a normal trial or difficulty. Life comes with challenges just by its nature. That's not what I mean by a spiritual crisis. A spiritual crisis takes place when God puts you in a situation only He can fix. When He places you in a scenario you can't buy your way out of, negotiate your way out of, or find someone to get you out of it, you know this is a spiritual crisis. Essentially, God has boxed you in.

What's more, in a situation like this, if God doesn't come through for you, you're sunk.

That is exactly where the Israelites find themselves as we continue our walk through the Hall of Heroes. Either God is going to bail them out of their difficulties or they will drown under them—literally.

It's interesting to note that, at this point in the exhibits, we see a switch from a person to a people group. That's because the author of Hebrews does that. In the midst of individual hero descriptions, he switches to the Israelites. That reveals that not only is it critical for us to live with individual faith but to learn to live with collective faith as well. What we do as a people group, or as a body of kingdom followers, will impact us too.

What we do personally matters. But what we do collectively also matters.

Sometimes we forget that one person's actions impact those around them, but the actions of a group of people leave an even larger ripple on the waters of our world events. To emphasize this, we now enter the next exhibit in the Hall of Heroes and are introduced to a unique chronicle of events—the collective choices of the Israelites, their steps of faith, many of which came with risk.

We start by reading Hebrews 11:28-30 inscribed on a wall:

> By faith [Moses] kept the Passover and the sprinkling of the blood, so that he who destroyed the firstborn would not touch them. By faith [the Israelites] passed through the Red Sea as though they were passing through dry land; and the Egyptians, when they attempted it, were drowned. By faith the walls of Jericho fell down after they had been encircled for seven days.

Notice that the beginning of this passage transitions from talking about Moses to talking about the Israelites in the same sentence. This is important, because Moses' faith was to set the precedent for an entire group of people and how they were to look to God. Following his 40 years as a shepherd, his experience with God at the burning bush, and his return to Egypt to lead his people to freedom, Moses had risen to a position of prominence among the Hebrew people. His faith had grown and developed personally in that time, and as a result, his had become an influential faith for others, encouraging them to take steps of faith.

Let's examine four of those steps.

Posting the Blood of Lambs

It was now Moses' role to convince an entire people group to put the blood of a lamb on their doorposts so the angel of death would pass over them. Keep in mind, this was an unprecedented instruction. The Israelites had never been told to do this. They could have argued and said the instruction seemed weird, let alone grotesque. But they didn't. They took a risk. They acted in true faith.

Faith is acting on something based on your belief that the one who told you to do it is telling the truth. In this case, the Israelites had witnessed the previous nine plagues. They'd seen that what Moses said would happen, according to God, actually happened. So they believed him. Because of their trust, they put the blood on their doorposts. The power of the Israelites' faith in the blood, made manifest through their obedient actions, kept their firstborns alive while the firstborns of the Egyptians all died that night.

Leaving All They Knew

Following this first faith step by the Israelites, God led them to an even greater risk. This showed up when they'd left Egypt and were headed toward the promised land.

For those of you unfamiliar with the context of this event, the Israelites had been slaves in Egypt for hundreds of years. When God sent the angel of death to slay the firstborn of the Egyptians and the firstborn of their cattle, the Egyptians urged the Israelites to leave and to leave quickly. They'd experienced enough of God's wrath. Exodus 12:33-36 gives us a glimpse into their departure.

> The Egyptians urged the people, to send them out of the land in haste, for they said, "We will all be dead." So the people took their dough before it was leavened, with their kneading bowls bound up in the clothes on their shoulders. Now the sons of Israel had done according to the word of Moses, for they had requested from the Egyptians articles of silver and articles of gold, and clothing; and the LORD had given the people favor in the sight of the Egyptians, so that they let them have their request. Thus they plundered the Egyptians.

Again, the Israelites had been slaves. But God had shown up so mightily in their deliverance that those who had once held them captive practically begged them to leave. Not only that, but they wanted them gone so badly that they gave them silver, gold, and clothing to help them on their way. That ought to shed some light on just how fast God can change a situation. Overnight, the Israelites went from slaves with nothing to a free and wealthy group of people. They were celebrating, singing, dancing, and filled with great joy as they headed out of Egypt (Exodus 15:1-21).

But they forgot one thing: They'd left all they knew, but they'd been reluctant to go.

Moving Forward (Eventually)

We'll explore this third step of faith more at length.

Before long, the Israelites' dancing had turned to dread. Shortly after they left, the king of Egypt regretted allowing his labor force to flee. He had a change of heart and decided to set out after them in order to bring them back. To do so, Pharaoh rounded up thousands of men and 600 chariots to chase after them. What's more, God encouraged him to do it. We know about God's intentional plan to have the Israelites backed into a corner because He tells us about it in Exodus 14:1-4:

> Now the LORD spoke to Moses, saying, "Tell the sons of Israel to turn back and camp before Pi-hahiroth, between Migdol and the sea; you shall camp in front of Baal-zephon, opposite it, by the sea. For Pharaoh will say of the sons of Israel, 'They are wandering aimlessly in the land; the wilderness has shut them in.' Thus I will harden Pharaoh's heart, and he will chase after them; and I will be honored through Pharaoh and all his army, and the Egyptians will know that I am the LORD." And they did so.

God set them up. There's no other way to interpret that passage. God had the Israelites wander around long enough that Pharaoh would think they were lost, confused, and vulnerable. Then He hardened Pharaoh's heart to pursue them. To harden a heart means to make it more intent on what the person had set their mind on doing in the first place. Essentially, God told Pharaoh, "Yay! Go get them!"

I'm sure that doesn't make sense to a lot of you. If God is good and the deliverer we're to look to, why did He lead the Israelites straight into a mess? Maybe you've asked this same question about your own life at times. Has it ever seemed like God is more on your unsaved employer's side than yours? Or on your unsaved coworker's side more than yours? Or even on your unsaved family members' side more than yours? You're praying to God and looking for Him to intervene on your behalf, but it just seems like the problem you're praying against only picks up speed in pursuit of you.

This is exactly what happened to the Israelites. They were set free only to become a target of Pharaoh's increased rage.

When the Israelites saw the chariots chasing after them, they did what most people would do. They forgot the lessons of the past demonstrating the faithfulness of God and became afraid. They quickly gave in to their despair and replaced faith with blame.

As we enter further into the exhibit, we hear the murmuring and complaining of frightened people. One voice stands out above them all as we hear these words once spoken to Moses:

> Is it because there were no graves in Egypt that you have taken us away to die in the wilderness? Why have you dealt with us in this way, bringing us out of Egypt? Is this not the word that we spoke to you in Egypt, saying, "Leave us alone that we may serve the Egyptians"? For it would have been better for us to serve the Egyptians than to die in the wilderness (Exodus 14:11-12).

In short, the Israelites said to Moses, "We told you so!" They'd told him to leave them alone as slaves, when at least they had homes and food to eat. They hadn't wanted to take a risk in order to go after a potential but, to them, highly suspicious reward. Sure, they were happy when things looked like they were going to work out, but as soon as it all went south, their cheers turned to complaints.

Moses sought to calm their fears by what he said next. As we stand in the exhibit facing a wall of water with nowhere to go, his voice rings out with what was recorded for us in verses 13-14:

> Do not fear! Stand by and see the salvation of the LORD which He will accomplish for you today; for the Egyptians whom you have seen today, you will never see them again forever. The LORD will fight for you while you keep silent.

The space we're in becomes eerily silent because Moses had just told everyone to shut their mouths. Moses didn't want to hear millions of people crying out to him at one time. His heart was burdened by their situation. He had eyes to see that there was nowhere to go, and they'd been led into an impossible situation. He told them to stop complaining and trust God.

But this brings us to the one missing verse in the Bible. You may not have known there was a missing verse in Scripture, but there is. This is because just after Moses told the Israelites to calm down, sit down, and watch what God would do, God responds to Moses. Verse 15 says, "Then the LORD said to Moses, 'Why are you crying out to Me? Tell the sons of Israel to go forward.'"

In verses 13-14, Moses is the confident preacher telling the Israelites to settle down. He's telling them God is going to fix this. He's talking his God-talk with ease and power. But in verse 15, God is chastising Moses for crying out to Him. Now, nowhere is it recorded that Moses cried out to God. Rather, all we're shown is Moses seeking to calm his people, which is why I call this a missing verse. If it were included, the passage might read something like this:

> Verses 13-14: "Fear not, God is going to deliver us!"
>
> Missing verse: "God, You better come here and do something, because I'm here telling Your people that You're going to do something. I told them You are the Wheel in the middle of a wheel, the Rose of Sharon, and the Balm in Gilead. I did what You asked me to do. But now You better do something because I put my neck on the line for You!"
>
> Verse 15: "Calm down, Moses. I've got this."

To be honest, this scenario feels all too familiar to me as a preacher. Maybe in your spiritual walk, as you seek to lead those around you or model what it means to live out the Christian faith, it seems familiar to you as well. I'll admit I've sometimes been preaching something publicly and simultaneously had a private conversation with God. I'm laying out the truths and principles for all to hear, but as I do, I'm inwardly asking Him, *Why aren't You showing up in my own life in these ways, and will You show up so I don't look like a fool up here by what I'm saying You will do!*

I understand the fear Moses was feeling in that moment. In fact, this reminds me of a time in our church's history when I was fully convinced God was going to give us a 65-acre plot of land adjacent to where our church sits now. I had my eye on that land, and I wanted it for our Master Plan. I just knew God would give it to us because we would use it to expand our kingdom footprint in the region in order to impact more lives for Him.

So I took a whole group of people from our congregation to walk the 65 acres together. I was so convinced in my spirit that our buying that land was God's plan that I had encouraged everyone to step foot on the land with me. In order to let God know we believed He would give the land to us, I wanted us to walk on it as Joshua was told to walk the promised land in Joshua 1:3.

After we'd walked for quite some time, I gathered everyone in a circle, and then we held hands and thanked God in advance for making the way for us to acquire this land possible. We had made an offer to buy it a few days before, and hundreds of congregants stood there with me as I led them in a confident, heartfelt prayer of thanksgiving for what God would do.

But what God did wasn't quite what I thought He would do. Before the week was out, the land had been sold to someone else.

As you might imagine, I felt like Moses in the missing verse. Questions rose in my spirit as I tried to figure out if I had misheard God's leading during my prayers. I sought to look within my own soul to see if there was any sin there that might have prevented this from coming about. Did I have pride in asking the congregation to confidently thank God for this land ahead of time? Or was that faith? Had the lines blurred between the two?

The more the questions ran through my mind, the more irritated I became. Nothing about God frustrates me more than when I believe Him for something and He chooses to do something else. It seemed like He had worked the whole plan against me. And now what was I supposed to do? I was a pastor shepherding a flock, teaching them to "trust in the Lord," all while they were looking at me like I was crazy!

I felt like Moses. Alone. Disappointed. Confused.

But wouldn't you know it, a couple of years later, I got a call that made all of my earlier questions disappear. The group that had purchased the land defaulted on their loan. The call was to ask us if we still wanted the land, and if so, we could have it at a much-reduced price.

God doesn't always open our Red Seas or feed our five thousands or topple our giants right when we want Him to. That's why faith is so risky. We're not only relying on Him for His ability to pull things off but learning how to trust that He will do so at the right time, letting go of our own need for control.

Understandably so, Moses was scared and confused as the Israelites complained to him while Pharaoh's chariots chased in hot pursuit. And truth be told, maybe you feel like Moses right now. Maybe you're scared and confused with your back up against a wall. And I know many of us collectively in the body of Christ look around at the culture and the world and can grow fearful about the rapid deterioration taking place. Multiple situations and scenarios can breed fear, causing it to spread like wildfire across our souls. But when that occurs, we need to turn to God like Moses did.

The missing verse isn't there to tell us what Moses said, but we know he cried out to God because God told him to stop it. He commanded him to stop rehashing his fears and instead do what He told him to do *in faith*.

Moses was then instructed to lift his staff and lead his people to safety, like God had asked him to do all along. We hear the next part of the passage coming from the loudspeaker above us in a deep, commanding voice.

> As for you, lift up your staff and stretch out your hand over the sea and divide it, and the sons of Israel shall go through the midst of the sea on dry land (verse 16).

Essentially, God instructed Moses to close his mouth just like Moses had told the Israelites to close theirs. There is a time for prayer, certainly, but also a time for action. God gave Moses the green light to move forward. So he did. He raised his staff, and the sea divided on its own.

Now the wall in front of us splits in two, both sides opening to reveal a passageway to another room. The floor beneath us looks like ground that was once wet and muddy but has hardened enough to walk on. It's uneven but easy enough to navigate. On each side of the passage stands a wall of water containing marine life for all to see. Our walk between them is awe-inspiring and alarming at the same time. But we make it through just like the Israelites did that day.

Is God waiting on you to take a risk with Him? Many of us are waiting on God when God is waiting on us. Sure, we may be praying, but prayer on its own isn't faith. Faith requires footsteps. Faith requires action. When Moses lifted his rod, God brought about a dual miracle. First, He held back the Red Sea, and second, He dried the muddy, wet ground once covered by water and made it hard enough for the Israelites, their wagons, and their animals to cross. Everyone could travel safely through the splitting of the sea because God hardened the ground beneath them.

What's more, once the Israelites had safely passed through, God lured the Egyptians onto the same path, only to close the waters over them. As the walls of this exhibit close behind us, we see an animated scene with the sides of the sea crashing back together, covering thousands of Egyptians and their horses and chariots. The roar of water splashing and cascading back into place fills the room, and then the wall lights up with these words over the settled sea:

> The LORD said to Moses, "Stretch out your hand over the sea so that the waters may come back over the Egyptians, over their chariots and their horsemen." So Moses stretched out his hand over the sea, and the sea returned to its normal state at daybreak, while the Egyptians were fleeing right into it; then the LORD overthrew the Egyptians in the midst of the sea. The waters returned and covered the chariots and the horsemen, even Pharaoh's entire

army that had gone into the sea after them; not even one of them remained (verses 26-28).

The Israelites had not only witnessed God drying the land for their deliverance but His returning the waters to their original place in order to drown those who pursued them. They were able to witness this because they had been willing, albeit grudgingly, to step out in faith. To take a risk with God.

If you never take a risk with God, you'll never see what He can do when only He can do it. Perhaps that's why God may not seem so real in your life—you've never risked everything on Him. You may be comfortable obeying Him on the little things, but you've never risked it all when you've been stuck between a rock and a hard place or He has you out on the edge of a cliff. God will show up and do miraculous things in your life if you step out in faith, but first you must trust Him enough to move when He says to move.

Why does God want to put you in a between-a-rock-and-a-hard-place situation to begin with? Because when He delivers you, He will be honored. God tells us that in verse 18, before the whole Red Sea scenario takes place. He didn't hide His reason for the Red Sea test: "Then the Egyptians will know that I am the LORD, when I am honored through Pharaoh, through his chariots and his horsemen." God reveals His power and His strength in cooperation with the kingdom heroes who will step out in faith in order that He may extend and expand His glory on earth. God wanted the Egyptians to know that He is the Lord.

Obeying God at Jericho

I'm sure that, through their experience at the Red Sea, the Israelites' level of faith increased, solidifying God as Lord in their hearts. But before we enter our next exhibit, we have one more display to explore. It's about a fourth step of faith the Israelites took—this time at Jericho.

Jericho was a walled city, fortified to such a degree that it was nearly impregnable by humanity. The walls were so high and so wide that people could conduct chariot races on top of them. The city was locked up tight like a drum. Yet here came the Israelites to invade it, according to God's plan. And God's plan was nothing anyone had ever envisioned.

You probably already know the story, but it's important to briefly take a look at it here. I'll go into more details on the battle of Jericho in the next chapter as we explore the life of a woman named Rahab, but let's first read about the military approach as recorded in Joshua 6:1-5:

> Jericho was tightly shut because of the sons of Israel; no one went out and no one came in. The LORD said to Joshua, "See, I have given Jericho into your hand, with its king and the valiant warriors. You shall march around the city, all the men of war circling the city once. You shall do so for six days.
>
> "Also seven priests shall carry seven trumpets of rams' horns before the ark; then on the seventh day you shall march around the city seven times, and the priests shall blow the trumpets. It shall be that when they make a long blast with the ram's horn, and when you hear the sound of the trumpet, all the people shall shout with a great shout; and the wall of the city will fall down flat, and the people will go up every man straight ahead."

In this battle plan, God gave Joshua a strategy no military leader had ever thought of before—or since, probably because any troops would look like fools carrying it out. He told them to march around the wall for seven days, and on the seventh day, they were to go around it seven times. But, of course, let's not forget they were to also blow their trumpets and scream a shout of praise!

Now, if you'd been looking at normal instructions in the military manual, you never would have taken this kind of risk. It just wouldn't make any sense. But remember, when God puts you in a position that doesn't make sense, that's because He wants you to see that He *is* God. He wants you to experience the fact that He alone can deliver what seems undeliverable.

By this time in their faith journey, the Israelites didn't complain. Instead, they put on their marching boots and started walking. Finally, after a week, they blew their trumpets and screamed. And as we all know, the walls came tumbling down!

There's nothing like seeing God knock down something you can't knock down on your own or turn something around you can't turn around yourself—even if it means doing something strange. But that's what He will do once you get past the thought that what He asks you to do can only be classified as odd. While it isn't odd to God, it's odd to us because we don't have His viewpoint. We see things only through our finite, limited understanding. God sees the end from the beginning. He knows the intricacies of how creation works. He can pull off things we wouldn't even know to ask Him to do because the concept itself never crossed our mind. He can make a way out of no way, just as He did in Jericho.

This truth came to light not too long ago when I was asked to speak for the second time in Clovis, New Mexico. The first time had been a decade or so before. On that first trip, I'd been picked up at the airport by a man from the church where I'd be speaking.

I'd been invited there to encourage the leaders in the community to work together to make a positive impact in their area, and I was happy to hear this man sharing his church's vision for doing that. But then my eyes caught something out the window—an enormous, abandoned building. It looked like it had once been a thriving, central location.

I pointed to it and said, "There's your community center for outreach right there."

Now, this man had never met me before. He'd heard me preach, but outside of that he didn't know me personally. He could have thought I was nuts to make such a statement, but my spirit felt led to say something, so I did.

"What building?" he asked, his voice revealing a hesitancy toward what he'd just heard.

"That one," I said, pointing again. "The one that looks abandoned."

"Oh, that is abandoned. It used to be a hospital. But no one has used it for years."

"Well, you will, because that's your community center."

We drove on a bit further, talking about how the spiritual leaders in their area could get together to make a real and lasting impact. Then he dropped me off at my hotel. I later spoke at the event and left the next day. To be honest, I didn't give my statements about the abandoned building another thought. That is, until years later, when this same man called, asking me to come speak again. This time, though, I would be speaking at that once-abandoned building, since purchased and transformed into a community center.

This community center had garnered the support and interest of many of the churches in that area. They'd all worked together to transform it into a food pantry, pregnancy center, job placement center, and many other helpful initiatives that support a community in the name of Christ.

"So how did you get it?" I asked him when he picked me up for the second time.

"Well, I couldn't shake what you said. It kept coming up in different ways, and we all became convinced that the abandoned building was ours to transform. So we went to the city and asked what it would take for us to get it."

"What did they say?" I asked.

"They told us they'd sell it to us for a dollar!"

He laughed with the confidence of a kingdom hero who had seen God's hand himself. They'd bought that entire building and the land it sat on for a dollar. Then they turned it into a Christian witness for the city.

Their testimony reminds us, as we see in the Israelites' exhibit in the Hall of Heroes, that when God is ready to move, He can turn things on a dime—or a dollar, for that matter. He can twist what He needs to and transform any situation to fit His intended goals for advancing His kingdom agenda on earth.

That's the issue with too many believers today—they just don't know who they're dealing with. It's not hard to be a kingdom hero when you realize who's on your side. When God has your back, it doesn't matter that it's against a wall. Just say the word (or blow the trumpet), and that wall will fall faster than a deck of cards stacked high.

What you and I need to take away from our visit to the Hall of Heroes is the assurance that when we do things God's way, according to His will, there really are no limits to what He can and will pull off in our lives. As He tells us in Isaiah 55:8-9, His ways are higher than our ways, and His thoughts are higher than our thoughts.

God is the King of kingdom heroes, calling each of us to rise, assemble, and usher in a new season of good, grace, and peace in our world as we take the risk of faith in our God, who can be trusted.

RAHAB,
A WOMAN
WHO PLEASED GOD

In the previous chapters, we've walked through the Hall of Heroes, taking a look at the various men and women who lived their lives according to the principles of heroic faith. As we now near the end of the great hall found in Hebrews 11, displaying the kingdom heroes of our past, we come upon a most unlikely candidate for an exhibit. After all the statues, sculptures, memorials, and elaborate models depicting mighty feats of heroic faith, you might initially think this woman doesn't belong. Perhaps the curator got something wrong. After all, the entryway to her exhibit says *Rahab, the Harlot.*

A harlot? Yes. That's the correct term to describe her. Not only that, but Rahab was a Gentile. She wasn't even an Israelite. By her nationality alone, she doesn't belong in a place dedicated to the heroic history of the Jewish people. Based on her historical background, she belongs to their enemies. After all, Rahab hailed from a family of pagan worship. The first two letters of her name were even chosen in honor of the Canaanite god, Ra. She'd been marked for his service at birth, branded for idolatry. Her parents wanted her to be intimately connected with this pagan god.

Not only did Rahab grow up in a pagan family but she grew up in a pagan culture that knew no boundaries on immorality. Human sacrifice ran rampant. Prostitution permeated the land. Homosexuality had infiltrated the highest reaches of the pillars in society. Bestiality was commonplace. There was murder for sport, such as in gladiator-style games. Rahab's culture wasn't just a little bit different from the Israelites; it was entirely different.

In addition, as we saw earlier, she herself was a harlot. Some probably called her a whore, or a madam, or an escort. Her occupation involved servicing men or women the sexual pleasures they craved. To say that this lady of the evening seems like an unlikely candidate for a faith-based hall of heroes is an understatement.

But regardless of what we might think after our initial peek at her exhibit, she's in there. Her statue stands tall yet alluring. She's clothed in the typical garments of her profession, with a sweeping scarf draped over her head in a seductive manner.

In our last exhibit we saw that God gave the Israelites instructions for how to topple the impregnable walls encircling Jericho. Situated behind her statue, we see a replica of the collapsed walls, looking like a tornado has torn through the city. Only one portion of the walls remains erect—the one just behind the statue of Rahab. Near the top of it we can see a red cloth hanging out a solitary window. That's where Rahab lived and worked. Her house had literally been built into the wall near the entrance gate, a prime location making it easily accessible and for visitors both local and otherwise to come in and out undetected by others.

Faced with Dilemma

As we walk further through Rahab's exhibit, we learn more about the biblical context of her story. It's embroidered in beautiful gold silk thread on a large, multicolored linen cloth hanging on the wall.

> Then Joshua the son of Nun sent two men as spies secretly from Shittim, saying, "Go, view the land, especially Jericho." So they went and came into the house of a harlot whose name was Rahab, and lodged there. It was told the king of Jericho, saying, "Behold, men from the sons of Israel have come here tonight to search out the land." And the king of Jericho sent word to Rahab, saying, "Bring out the men who have come to you, who have entered your house, for they have come to search out all the land."

But the woman had taken the two men and hidden them, and she said, "Yes, the men came to me, but I did not know where they were from. It came about when it was time to shut the gate at dark, that the men went out; I do not know where the men went. Pursue them quickly, for you will overtake them."

But she had brought them up to the roof and hidden them in the stalks of flax which she had laid in order on the roof. So the men pursued them on the road to the Jordan to the fords; and as soon as those who were pursuing them had gone out, they shut the gate (Joshua 2:1-7).

The accessibility of Rahab's home was why the Israelites were able to send two spies to her, to ascertain the information they needed in their reconnaissance. Mural images on both sides of the hanging cloth first show the two men sneaking into Rahab's home and then someone spying them and reporting them to the king. We also see the king sending word to Rahab to turn over the enemies' spies and her pretending not to know what he's talking about. She's saying to the men he sent that the spies have already left even though she's hidden them on the roof. We can see them hiding if we look closely enough, toward the top of the mural.

Rahab lied.

Now, if you're still scratching your head, wondering why Rahab is in the Hall of Heroes—especially because she's not only a harlot but a liar as well—let's examine what the Scriptures show us about a choice we sometimes must make.

Make the Choice That Brings God Glory

We all know lying is a sin; the Bible tells us lying is a sin. But Rahab knew turning these two men in as spies would get them killed. She was faced with two wrong actions: lie, saving the men's lives, or tell the truth, turning them in to be killed. She decided to lie, and in a moment we'll see why she made that decision.

A similar thing happened when Pharaoh instructed midwives to kill newborn Hebrew babies (Exodus 1:15-22). They had two bad options:

lie to Pharaoh and save the babies or kill the babies as Pharaoh instructed. Scripture tells us they chose to lie because they "feared God":

> The midwives feared God, and did not do as the king of Egypt had commanded them, but let the boys live. So the king of Egypt called for the midwives and said to them, "Why have you done this thing, and let the boys live?" The midwives said to Pharaoh, "Because the Hebrew women are not as the Egyptian women; for they are vigorous and give birth before the midwife can get to them." So God was good to the midwives, and the people multiplied, and became very mighty. Because the midwives feared God, He established households for them (verses 17-21).

If two sins are the only options before you, you are to choose the one that will bring God the greatest glory. You have to carry out the one that will honor Him the most. Rahab chose to hide the spies and lie to the king's messengers to make them pursue the men away from where they could be found. She chose to save their lives.

Now, the reason Rahab did this, and the reason we see her in the Hall of Heroes, is revealed to us as we round the corner and come to the next portion of Scripture on a second linen cloth hanging on a wall. It's taken from Joshua 2:8-11.

> Before they lay down, she came up to them on the roof, and said to the men, "I know that the LORD has given you the land, and that the terror of you has fallen on us, and that all the inhabitants of the land have melted away before you. For we have heard how the LORD dried up the water of the Red Sea before you when you came out of Egypt, and what you did to the two kings of the Amorites who were beyond the Jordan, to Sihon and Og, whom you utterly destroyed. When we heard it, our hearts melted and no courage remained in any man any longer because of you; for the LORD your God, He is God in heaven above and on earth beneath."

Essentially, Rahab let the men know she knew their God was the real deal. His reputation had reached their city walls. Her people had been told about the miraculous deliverance out of Egypt. They'd heard of the parting of the Red Sea. The Israelites had become known as a people whose God worked wonders on their behalf.

Based on her role in the community and location near the city gate, I'm sure Rahab was in a position to hear a lot of things. Rulers in a city during that time often congregated in the vicinity of a city gate, which might also be why Rahab had made her home there. The information Rahab and the others she worked with had heard was to be taken seriously. Her sources were reliable. So, as a result of what she'd heard, Rahab chose to flip. She chose to jump sides. She made the faith decision to align herself with the one, true God.

Now, Rahab stood alone in this choice. She and her friends and associates had all heard the same things about the Hebrews' God, but only Rahab chose to make a move based on what they'd heard. She was the one who made a radical decision to get out of danger while she could.

Rahab's story reminds us that sometimes siding with God means siding against the culture or the world in which we live. But every serious kingdom follower eventually reaches a point where they have to choose Christ or choose the crowd. You have to choose God or the group. You must choose between the King or the culture. This might show up on your job, with your friends, or even with a dating relationship or within your family. Whatever the case, your choice will reveal your faith because it will reveal your loyalty and allegiance.

We covered this when we explored the exhibit on Moses, but when you align with God, you *will* suffer some level of persecution. Again, Scripture clearly tells us that all those who live godly in Christ Jesus will (2 Timothy 3:12). You may feel like the lone man or the lone woman when you make a faith decision, but oftentimes those faith decisions are a matter of life and death. Had Rahab sided with the culture, she would have gone down with the walls. She and her family would have lost their lives the day those trumpets blew. But because she chose to place her faith in the God she'd heard about only from a distance, she saved both herself and her family.

Now, Rahab had to have been a clever lady to last long in the business she was in. She knew how to negotiate. She knew how to maneuver. She knew the art of a deal, which is exactly what she did in cutting a deal with the spies. If you'll look behind you to the other side of the room we've just entered, you'll see the next part of her story, where Rahab's negotiation skills take center stage.

The Kindness of God's Divine Covering

On a large display that looks like one of the mammoth stones that once stood as part of Jericho's walls are carved these words. They come from Rahab.

> "Please swear to me by the LORD, since I have dealt kindly with you, that you also will deal kindly with my father's household, and give me a pledge of truth, and spare my father and my mother and my brothers and my sisters, with all who belong to them, and deliver our lives from death." So the men said to her, "Our life for yours if you do not tell this business of ours; and it shall come about when the LORD gives us the land that we will deal kindly and faithfully with you" (verses 12-14).

Rahab is shrewd. She knows what's about to happen in her land, and she believes the reputation of the God she's heard about. And even though her countrymen feel secure behind fortified walls, she doesn't. She's heard the stories of the God who can divide an entire sea with His wind. So she tells the two Israelite spies what she will do for them and then expresses the specific covering she wants in return for her actions. She cuts a deal based on a decision rooted in faith.

What Rahab receives as part of the deal is the kindness of divine covering. The word used for "kindly" in this passage we just read is the Hebrew word *chessed*.* It means "faithfulness, loyalty." It was God's covenantal word for how He would cover His people. In the Old Testament, *chessed* is used over 240 times to define God's loyal love to His own. When Rahab made

---

* *Strong's Concordance of the Bible*, H2617.

a faith decision to ask for God's covering, she sought to transition herself from outside of His covenant to under it. This was an alignment choice, and a wise one at that. Rahab had chosen her words intentionally.

The problem with far too many believers today is that they seek to cut a deal that requires God to do His part first. But that's the opposite of faith. That's operating on sight. Rahab was willing to put herself and her family at risk because of her faith that God would be loyal in holding up His end of the bargain later. Her faith choice and actions preceded the conclusion of the deal.

Rahab's story further illustrates much of what I've already shared in this book. If you want God to do something for you, with you, by you, or through you, you need to act first. You first need to let Him know what you're willing to do for Him in faith. Because without faith it's impossible to please Him. He wants to see your steps of faith. He wants to witness the moves you make. And He's not going to show you what He's going to do until you walk forward. In doing so, you demonstrate your trust in His integrity.

God doesn't mind answering the prayers of His kingdom followers. He doesn't mind responding to our requests. In fact, He wants to do so. He wants to do things for us. But due to the nature of faith itself, we need to move before He does.

As the Israelites marched around the wall of Jericho for the first six days, I'm sure the conversations within the wall were nothing short of mockery. Yet Rahab stayed true to her beliefs and never caved to a culture of "impolite memes" and insults. She stood strong. She stood tall. Thus, when the wall eventually did fall, she was one of the last few standing.

As I mentioned near the start of this chapter, Rahab's home was *in* the wall. And we all know the walls of Jericho collapsed, as recorded in Scripture. But due to God's loyal covenantal covering of love, one portion of the wall remained intact—the portion that housed Rahab near the gate. Rahab got her miracle covering by God when He delivered her and her family due to her actions of faith. She trusted Him in advance of the crisis, so that when the crisis took place, she and her family were safe.

The Rest of Rahab's Story

Now, all that would be good enough for Rahab to be inducted into the Hall of Heroes. Hers is a great story of deliverance. But that isn't the end of her story. As we keep walking through the exhibit, we see a lot more because Rahab keeps showing up in Scripture. She didn't just appear in the book of Joshua and then leave the scene. We also read about her, indirectly, in 1 Chronicles 2:51, where we learn about her husband Salmon's trade. That verse tells us he was the "father of Bethlehem." That means he designed and built the entire city, which also means he must have been wealthy and influential among the Israelites. Thus, Rahab not only escaped certain death by her faith decision but positioned herself to fall in love with and marry an affluent man in her new culture.

How do we know Salmon was her husband? Because of Matthew 1:5-6, where they both show up in the lineage of Jesus Christ: "Salmon was the father of Boaz by Rahab, Boaz was the father of Obed by Ruth, and Obed the father of Jesse. Jesse was the father of David the king." Thus, we see that Rahab the prostitute became Rahab the proselyte who married into an upscale family in Israel, only to later become the great-great-grandmother of King David. She's recorded in Scripture as part of the high-class ladies in the lineage of Jesus Christ!

Now, if God can take a prostitute and get her married to someone special while using her to become part of the lineage of our Savior Himself, He can do anything with anyone. Her exhibit should be an encouragement for everyone who walks through it, and I hope it's an encouragement to you.

I don't know what you may have done or how long you've done it. I don't know what thoughts and emotions have held you back from stepping forward in faith. But I do know your past doesn't have to determine your future. Whatever you did back in the day, or even if you're still caught up in it right now, if you'll allow yourself to align under the one, true God by choosing Him over the culture and the crowd, you'll discover that He is a master at taking a mess and turning it into a miracle.

Do not give up. Do not give in to the lies that say you're too far gone for God to use you as a kingdom hero. If God could help Rahab get a fresh start, regain her dignity, and establish a new status and a lasting legacy, He can do the same with you.

Move Those Feet

Not only did Rahab show up in the lineage of Jesus Christ but she showed up in the book of James as an example to all of us—an example for what faith truly looks like. As James wrote to the believers about the concept of faith being dead without works, he was led by the Spirit to include Rahab as an illustration of just that. After he reminded his readers about Abraham and his great faith, James wrote,

> You see that a man is justified by works and not by faith alone. In the same way, was not Rahab the harlot also justified by works when she received the messengers and sent them out by another way? For just as the body without the spirit is dead, so also faith without works is dead (James 2:24-26).

Rahab is held up as a strong example of a profoundly critical theological concept called "justification by works." This isn't to be confused with justification by faith, which leads to salvation as recorded in Romans 3 and 4. Each of us is to trust in Christ alone as our sin-bearer for the forgiveness of our sins and believe in Him for the gift of eternal life. That justification has been established for us for free, based on what Jesus did for us on the cross. We are justified for eternal salvation apart from works, free of charge, and based on both grace and mercy through the shed blood of Jesus.

But that's not what James is talking about when he mentions Abraham and Rahab as examples of faith. He's writing about a justification by works, which brings heaven's authority to bear on our earthly experiences. Justification by faith gets a person to heaven. Justification by works gets heaven to intervene in the affairs of humanity on earth. Justification by faith is demonstrated through faith alone in Christ alone. Justification by works is demonstrated by function based on faith.

Rahab's decision to hide the spies and send them out of the city another way so they wouldn't get caught not only saved them but led to God saving her and her family as well. Doing so freed up God to respond to her in history. And when you and I declare, as Rahab did, that we're going to make our choices based on our belief system of faith in God—even if that means going against our culture and the crowd—we'll see God's hand move in our lives like never before. We'll see Him visit us in history in ways we could never have imagined. If He did it for Rahab, He can do it for us. Her story is a story for all of us.

What God Wills for You Despite Your Past

It's interesting that whenever Rahab shows up in Scripture, whether it's in Matthew, James, or Hebrews, her past occupation as a harlot is mentioned right next to her name. No one else is referenced in a way that ties their career to their name. We don't read *Peter, the fisherman* every time he appears. But we do read *Rahab, the harlot*. Obviously, God wanted us to remember who Rahab was, because her transformation from a harlot to a hero ought to inspire all of us to know that He can redeem everyone who humbles themselves before Him. As I've said before, no one is too far gone.

When I preached a message on Rahab, the harlot, to my local congregation, I brought a $100 bill with me to the pulpit. Toward the end of the sermon, I pulled it out of my pocket and held it up, asking if anyone wanted it. As you might imagine, all hands went up. But then I did something no one anticipated. I wadded the $100 bill in my fist in a tight ball, and then I dropped it onto the floor and stepped on it. Now not only was it crumpled and wrinkled but dirty.

Picking it back up, I asked the congregation if anyone wanted it now. The same hands went up. That was because even though the $100 bill I now held in my hands was messed up, crushed, and filthy, it had not lost its value. It was still worth every bit of $100.

But before someone could run up to the pulpit to grab the bill from my hand, I tore it in two. Then, holding up both pieces, I asked the congregation if anyone still wanted this crushed, dirty, and torn-in-two $100 bill. Every single hand raised before went up again. That was because with just a little bit of tape, that $100 bill would still hold its value. The value was intrinsic to what it was.

I don't care how your past may have crushed you, wrinkled you, dirtied you, or torn you from the floor up, in the right hands you retain every bit of your value. You are made in the image of the King Himself. In reminding us of Rahab's occupation over and over again, God wanted us to know that no matter how bad our past may be, if we choose Him by faith—over the crowd, circumstances, popularity, fear, money, and more—He will restore us with His kindness. He will offer us His loving, covenantal covering. He will give us back the years the locusts may have stolen (Joel 2:25). And He will transform the shame of the past into the dignity of a brighter tomorrow.

In short, you can be a kingdom hero too.

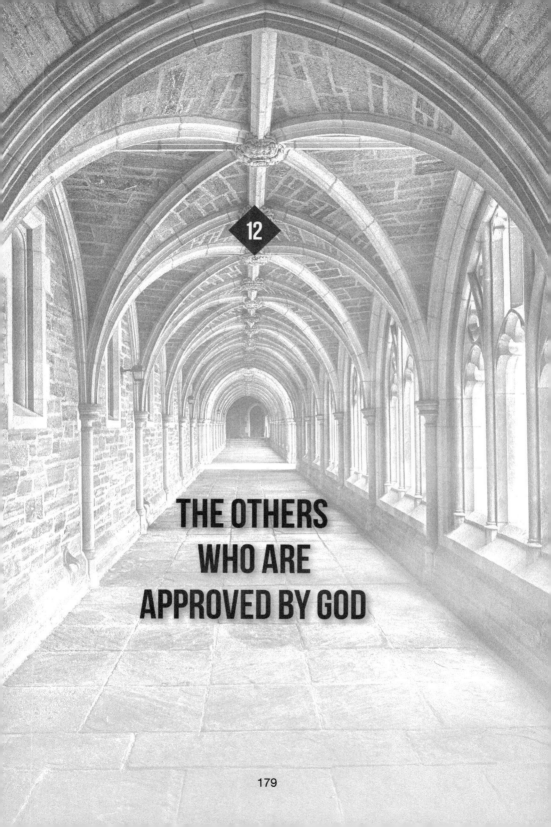

12

THE OTHERS
WHO ARE
APPROVED BY GOD

We're nearing the end of our tour through the Hall of Heroes, and it's been a great experience so far. As we visited each exhibit, we learned what it looks like to live our life by faith. We saw men and women who did just that and whose lives can encourage you and me to do the same. Living a life of faith is a daily decision that activates the hand and movement of the power and presence of God in our lives.

Let's summarize what we've covered so far.

Hebrews 11:6 makes it crystal clear that without faith we won't see God. This is because without faith, we do not please Him. The absence of faith results in the absence of the manifest presence of God. In other words, we will know He exists, but we won't necessarily experience His existence in our day-to-day life. That's why in Scripture God so often urges us to live our lives by faith. He wants us to experience Him. He desires to intervene in our situations. He wants to reveal His power in our circumstances. But that requires our faith to participate in the process of His providential hand.

As a reminder, faith is acting like it is so even when it's not so, so it might be so simply because God said so. Faith is verifiable. You never have to wonder if you have faith because it shows up in your feet. It shows up in your walk, not just your talk. It's made real when you choose to obey God even when you don't see the reality or rationale of your obedience from a human perspective.

What's more, faith must always precede sight. Once you have sight, it's no longer faith. That's why Hebrews 11:1 declares, "Faith is the assurance of things hoped for, the conviction of things not seen." If you have to see it first, you've canceled faith. Faith is prior to and apart from sight. In fact, faith leads to sight. But even so, most people decide what they're going to do by what they see first. As a result, they regularly cancel the supernatural from taking place in their lives.

The African impala is a magnificent animal. I got to see one on a trip Lois and I took to South Africa several years ago. The African impala can jump ten feet straight up in the air. It can also jump outwardly up to 30 feet. Yet if you put an African impala with all of its beauty, power, and ability behind a three-foot-high wall, expecting it to leap over it high and long, it will remain imprisoned there for life. This is due to one flaw: It won't jump if it can't see where it will land. Thus it limits its own movements to its sight. While the ability is there to become free, it won't exercise that ability because it won't trust what it cannot see.

Many of us are similarly controlled by circumstances we let imprison us behind our own walls of fear, uncertainty, and doubt. The devil uses them to keep us trapped, knowing that far too many of us feel the need to see before we set out. Yet faith doesn't operate that way. Faith operates on the basis of belief.

Do We Get It Yet?

By the time we near the end of Hebrews 11, the author has rehearsed this concept so many times that you almost sense an air of impatience seeping into his words. I love how Hebrews 11:32 opens with a hint of honest frustration: "What more shall I say?" The author has already written 31 verses, giving examples of great heroes of the faith and what they were able to achieve by faith. It's almost as if he's shrugging his shoulders in exasperation, saying, "What else do you need to get this?"

Whenever I read the start of that verse, I'm reminded of the song "If You Don't Know Me by Now." The lyrics convey that if the person to whom the words are spoken still doesn't understand the person who's speaking, they probably never will. It's almost as if the author of Hebrews is saying something similar to those who don't quite get it yet. After all, he's shown the readers what faith accomplishes in a person's life. But if they're still not motivated to live by faith, what more can he say?

He's like an old-time preacher who says, "If I only had a little bit more time, I could tell you so much more!" And then he goes on to tell you anyhow. In fact, that's what the author of Hebrews does. He goes on with a list of more people who lived by faith. We read this in the concluding verses of the chapter:

> Time will fail me if I tell of Gideon, Barak, Samson, Jephthah, of David and Samuel and the prophets, who by faith conquered kingdoms, performed acts of righteousness, obtained promises, shut the mouths of lions, quenched the power of fire, escaped the edge of the sword, from weakness were made strong, became mighty in war, put foreign armies to flight. Women received back their dead by resurrection... (verses 32-35).

Now, the author didn't go into details about these individuals like he did about the ones in the first 31 verses, but he does draw our attention to them. Here are brief summaries of their walks by faith.

Gideon

Gideon was a judge, but he was also a scared judge. He was even a passive guy in a lot of ways. But then God called on him because Israel was being invaded by the enemy. Even though Gideon was afraid, he amassed an army of 32,000 men.

But then God told him he had too many.

Of course, Gideon was confused. How could 32,000 men be too many when going up against an enormous army? But God knew better, and so he asked Gideon to shrink his army to just 300 men. Gideon may have felt lost by this point, wondering how he could secure a victory against tens of thousands with just 300 men. But that's when God reminded him it wasn't just 300 men. It was 300 men plus God. The "plus God" part would make the difference. Thus, Gideon dropped his logic. He dropped his dependence on his own reasoning. He let go of his battle plans and scheming and chose to obey God.

When Gideon obeyed God, he wound up routing his enemy. What's more, he did so with just 300 men. Lessons like these encourage us to do what God says to do, especially when we can't logically figure out how something will work. It's by faith that Gideon defeated an army even though he was scared and unprepared by the world's standards.

Barak

Now, if Gideon was scared, Barak was weak. He was a weak man who ran from difficulty and troubles. In fact, the only strength he had was from a woman named Deborah. Barak was too scared to go into battle himself, and he told Deborah he wouldn't go unless she went with him. As a result, Deborah had to do what many women have to do—hold up a man's hands when times get tough.

Thus, with the encouragement of Deborah, who transferred her faith in God to him, Barak went into battle and won. Even though he was a weak man, God used him by faith to trample the enemies of Israel.

Samson

So far we have Gideon who was scared and Barak who was weak. Next the author tells us about Samson, who was a player. Samson lived with extreme moral and passion issues. Yet even though he was a man who failed in this area, whenever he was willing to operate by faith in God, the supernatural would invade him and use him to accomplish God's will.

The Bible tells us he killed a thousand men with the jawbone of a donkey. He was a beast on the battlefield. What's more, he killed more of his enemies on the day of his death than he'd defeated in all his years. Samson went out in a blaze even though he struggled with real issues throughout his life. His usefulness to God's agenda never nullified the consequences of his issues, but it did allow God to show up when the Israelites needed Him the most.

Jephthah

Next up on the list of heroes is Jephthah. Jephthah didn't come from a heritage of honor. He was the son of a prostitute (Judges 11:1-3). His father had hooked up with a whore and gotten her pregnant, and she gave birth to Jephthah. His father's other sons, by his wife, didn't want anything to do with Jephthah. As soon as he was old enough to fend for himself, they ran him off.

To say that Jephthah had a questionable background is an understatement. He was illegitimate, rejected by his siblings, had a messed-up family, and was basically on his own. Yet when God went looking for someone to deliver His people, He went to Jephthah. Jephthah didn't allow his past to control his present. He chose to obey God. And because he did, he routed the enemies of God despite not having a stable background or firm footing.

David

Then there's David. David was young when God chose him. He was short. He was small. Yet none of this mattered when he went up against the giant named Goliath.

In 1 Samuel 17, we see he grabbed a sling shot and five smooth stones to go after his foe. Let me tell you, David was such a great shot that it took only one to bring the bully down. David knew the giant was not circumcised. He didn't look at his size. He looked at the fact that he hadn't been cut, and as a result, he did not fall under God's covering.

David never let the size of the battle determine where it wound up. He overcame all odds because of his great faith and heart after God.

Samuel

After David, the author of Hebrews mentions Samuel. Now, Samuel really struggled in his roles and responsibilities in life. He was a weak father who did not address his sons when they turned away from God during their own seasons of leadership to which he had appointed them (1 Samuel 8:1-3). Samuel definitely had some significant flaws as a dad. Yet when he was willing to operate by faith, God used him to anoint the king of Israel, who would set the nation on a spiritual course toward victory and strength.

As you can easily see, those who wound up in the Hall of Heroes were not pristine models of integrity. Every one of them had weaknesses and blind spots. Every one of them hadn't yet matured in some areas. Every one of them had places that needed to be shored up and tended to. Yet by their faith they achieved greatness. When they were willing to operate by faith, God used them to advance His kingdom agenda on earth.

The people in this Hall of Heroes ought to encourage you, because no matter what your yesterday may look like, if you live by faith today, God can use you tomorrow. But you must recognize that for you to achieve greatness in the kingdom of God, it must be done by faith. God must see you trust Him by your feet, not just by your feelings. He must witness your obedience in how you function.

One of the reasons God allows negative realities to enter our lives is to see whether we will face them with faith or seek to navigate them by sight. When you choose to face obstacles by faith, God joins you in that. But when you choose to face obstacles by sight, reflected by the decisions to operate with human wisdom, He lets you take care of them yourself.

As we saw earlier in the passage, faith enabled these individuals to conquer kingdoms, perform acts of righteousness, and obtain promises. Faith shut the mouths of lions. Faith quenched the power of the flame. Faith caused weak men to become strong, thus putting foreign armies to flight. Faith can route whole nations.

The Work of Faith

Sometimes we mix up salvation and faith's roles on a daily basis, so I want to set the record straight in a book focusing so strongly on faith. When you accept Jesus Christ as your personal Savior by placing your faith in Him alone for the forgiveness of your sins, you are given eternal life. But while you trust Christ *through* faith, you are now supposed to live your life *by* faith. These are two very different things. Trusting Christ for salvation is akin to receiving a gift. Living by faith is doing a work.

That's why James says faith without works is dead (James 2:14-26). He isn't talking about getting to heaven; he's talking about getting heaven down to you. Accepting Christ as your Savior takes you to heaven; living by faith brings heaven's power and God's experiential presence and authority to you on earth. It allows you to see God enter history by showing up in your circumstances. When you live by faith, God brings the supernatural to bear in the midst of the natural situations of your existence on earth.

Unfortunately, people often confuse these two things. As a result, many Christians don't live by faith, which has the accompaniment of works. Rather, they live by sight while calling it faith. They say they trust God to do it. They wait on God for every move. They resign themselves to living without movement or momentum, expecting God to do everything for them. Yet while God did everything for you and me through the gift of salvation, He does expect us to do the work of faith made manifest in obedience to Him throughout our lives.

Faith is so powerful that it can even flip the natural order of things. In Hebrews 11:35 we read that "women received back their dead by resurrection." This is referring to those who were brought back to life by Elijah and Elisha. Yet you and I will never get to see God flip the order of things in our lives if we continue to view life through the lens of this world's perspective.

Living by faith means acting before you see the result you desire. When you do, you get to experience God reversing things in your life that are humanly impossible to reverse.

Something Better on the Other Side

Before we get the idea that everything runs smoothly when we live by faith, the author of Hebrews wants to remind us of what many endure as a result of their faith. We pick up the passage in verses 35-38:

> Others were tortured, not accepting their release, so that they might obtain a better resurrection; and others experienced

mockings and scourgings, yes, also chains and imprisonment. They were stoned, they were sawn in two, they were tempted, they were put to death with the sword; they went about in sheepskins, in goatskins, being destitute, afflicted, ill-treated (men of whom the world was not worthy), wandering in deserts and mountains and caves and holes in the ground.

Granted, this is not the kind of testimony people want to hear. As we near the end of the Hall of Heroes and look at the walls with paintings around us, we see images of men and women tortured for their faith, experiencing mocking and scourging, or chained in imprisonment. Ahead of us are statues of those bent over as they're being stoned to death. To the right of them is a statue of someone whose tormentors are sawing him in two.

These scenes cause us to gasp. These aren't the hero stories we tell our children before putting them to bed. In fact, we don't even want to read these stories ourselves. How many of us have quickly glanced past these verses?

The truth is this—again based on 2 Timothy 3:12: Anyone who tells you living for Christ means you will not suffer is lying. Some of the faithful in the Bible were penalized for their beliefs. Some were killed for their stand. Some were mocked, scorned, rebuked, and left for dead. Yet despite it all, they remained committed. We know this because the author of Hebrews tells us they would not accept their release. They embraced their suffering, knowing it was being used to produce a greater reward. They embraced it "so that they might obtain a better resurrection." All believers don't transition into eternity equally.

See, what will give you the strength to take your stand for Christ even in the face of loss, persecution, and pain is seeing something better on the other side. One of the reasons people compromise their faith is that they don't believe something better is up ahead. But it's by faith that we find the fortitude necessary to face opposition. And while that something better may come to us in this life, it may not. It may come in heaven. Some heroes even faced and surrendered to death in order that they might experience heaven to the fullest.

We saw this play out in a man named Stephen, whose story is in Acts 7. When Stephen was being stoned to death for his faith in Jesus Christ, he looked up to heaven and saw Jesus standing on the right hand of the Father. Because he could see something better, he was willing to leave this world behind.

Believers ought to be able to die with dignity because, at the point of death, God gives approved believers who lived a life of faith a unique, dying grace. He often lets His faithful followers see something, know something, or feel something that assures them of His special presence. When that happens, those who are about to transition into Glory don't mind crossing to the other side. Fear is replaced with peace. That's why the apostle Paul could say this with such confidence: "With all boldness, Christ will even now, as always, be exalted in my body, whether by life or by death. For to me, to live is Christ and to die is gain" (Philippians 1:20-22).

The enemy wants to keep you from living by faith so you won't get to see anything better. And as long as you don't see anything better, you stay stuck where you are. You remain trapped in what your 20/20 vision can reveal to you, which isn't much. Yet once you learn to live by faith, God lets you see that He can resurrect situations, relationships, and even emotions you thought were dead and gone. But you'll experience a resurrection when you make a faith-based decision on what to do next.

Do What Living by Faith Takes

Many of you will never see financial victory in your family because you've chosen money over spiritual priority in the home. If you neglect your family while pursuing money, you'll wind up losing both. That's because you will have chosen to disregard God in your decision making. It doesn't matter how many church services you attend; without a visible, viable faith showing up in your actions, you will never experience God's greatest manifestations of His presence in your life. The financial scenario is just one category. You can pick any category, and the truth still applies. When you leave faith in God, as demonstrated by your disobedient actions, out of your independent decisions you wind up on the short end of your destiny every single time.

Now, I get it. I understand. Living by faith sometimes makes you come across as different. You may even appear weird to others like Noah did. But as we saw in verse 38, those who live by faith are those men and women of whom "the world was not worthy." What makes the world not worthy of certain people? When they live so high in the spiritual realm that those who physically live with them in the earthly realm rarely understand what they're doing. The physical world and her people think they're odd. They think they've lost their minds. They call them fanatics. Freaks. Or any other name people can come up with.

But the author of Hebrews reminds us the world, made up of those who live according to the precepts of worldliness, is not worthy of people who truly live by faith. It's not worthy of those who know how to function from a higher vantage point. Those who live with an eternal perspective outwit, outplay, and outlast those who don't.

That doesn't mean they will always get their rewards while on earth, but they will receive them on steroids in eternity. We witness this in these next verses from Hebrews 11:

> All these, having gained approval through their faith, did not receive what was promised, because God had provided something better for us, so that apart from us they would not be made perfect (verses 39-40).

You read that right. None of those just mentioned, who had gained approval through their faith, received what was promised in this life. In other words, many of the Old Testament saints did not get what they were looking for. For example, Abraham never got to own the land God promised him. He got to wander on it, but he never owned it. He got to see God work, but in his lifetime he didn't see everything God had promised him. The writer of Hebrews tells us the reason for this is that God was waiting for "us." The "us" in that verse refers to the New Testament Christians. It refers to you and me and all of us in the church age.

You and I have been gifted unique privileges those who walked this earth during the previous dispensation didn't have while living under the law. We get to experience the exciting benefits and privileges that are part of the new covenant. That being so, we ought to live with even more motivation than they did, because we are positioned to live out the fulfillment of God's promises right now. But we can live out the fulfillment of these promises only when we choose to trust God, even if we have to do so in the dark. Trusting God in the dark brings you and your present reality into the light.

When you choose to step out in obedience even though you don't know the result ahead of time, God will usher in the highest result according to His perfect plan. But you must step out in faith. You must take an action step toward His revealed will. His rewards don't come to you simply because you want them. They come as a result of making a decision to base your life choices on the truth and instruction of His Word. It is crucial to note that the ultimate goal of living by faith is divine approval. It means prioritizing the pleasing of God over the pleasing of people, and even pleasing yourself.

Look around again before we exit this exhibit. Some of the images you see of those being persecuted and oppressed on this earth have transformed. Now they're celebrating with Christ in the heavens. What's more, they're all looking down on you. They're watching you. Cheering for you, hopeful that you will have learned enough from their lives to encourage you to move forward in faith.

It's your turn. It's your move. It's your time to demonstrate a life of faith in Christ.

13

JOINING
THE
KINGDOM HEROES

Let's look at the year 2020 one more time.

It came at all of us with a mission. It had its own agenda. It was a unique year, no matter how you summarize it. It brought surprises, twists, limitations, and loss on an unusual scale. According to one study, the number of adults admittedly struggling with depression tripled during 2020.[*] This new number accounted for roughly a fourth of all American adults at that time. In addition, suicide rates soared during the onset of this season of uncertainty. As a pastor, I was inundated with calls, text messages, and requests for counseling from those who needed help. They needed hope. They were losing heart. And as I write this, in early 2021, many of those struggles continue.

For me personally, the onset of 2021 saw an increase in difficulties over the previous year. In mid-February, I was diagnosed with COVID-19. The timing couldn't have been worse. I was diagnosed just one day before a disastrous snow and ice storm hit Texas, knocking out power and water for millions. Roads were impassable. Power was intermittent. But God's grace was sufficient.

As I rested and recovered at home alone from moderate symptoms, I got news that our national ministry offices had experienced flooding. The

---

[*] Robby Berman, "US cases of depression have tripled during the COVID-19 pandemic," *Medical News Today*, September 19, 2020, https://www.medicalnewstoday.com/articles/us-cases-of-depression-have-tripled-during-the-covid-19-pandemic.

pipes above the ceiling, which serve as emergency water sources in case of a fire, had frozen and burst as the non-winterized state of Texas continued to reach subzero temperatures. All the offices flooded and then froze overnight. Ceilings caved in from the weight of the semisolid water and ice, destroying furniture, inventory, and much more. Not only that, but some of my family members' houses experienced flooding as well due to the loss of power and frozen pipes.

Obviously, 2020 didn't own a corner on troubles. If you are an occupant on planet Earth, troubles will come and difficulties will arise no matter what year you are in.

But as you've seen throughout our journey, the Hall of Heroes is made up of people who faced dire scenarios with a level of spiritual dignity. Many if not all felt like giving up at one point. They wanted to give in. It would have been easier to exit this world than to continue pushing through the difficulties that mounted upon them. But what makes them stand apart from all others and has placed them in this special chapter of the Bible, honoring their faith, is the fact that they remained steadfast to the end.

Their stories serve as an inspiration for us. They're meant to goad us toward our own goals of heroic faith. In fact, as we leave Hebrews 11 and turn the page to the next chapter, and as we enter the final corridor of the museum before we leave, we hear words summarizing why these kingdom heroes mean so much to us. We hear the charge for how their lives should impact our own. We receive our own commission to live as kingdom heroes in a broken world and establish our own statue in this hallowed museum.

Hebrews 12:1-3 phrases our calling like this:

> Since we have so great a cloud of witnesses surrounding us, let us also lay aside every encumbrance and the sin which so easily entangles us, and let us run with endurance the race that is set before us, fixing our eyes on Jesus, the author and perfecter of faith, who for the joy set before Him endured the cross, despising the shame, and has sat down at the right hand of the throne of God. For consider Him who has endured such hostility by

sinners against Himself, so that you will not grow weary and lose heart.

The bottom line? We are not to lose heart.

Let me help you with a picture of what it means to lose heart. Losing heart is like runners becoming exhausted to the point of collapse. They lose all strength, energy, and even motivation to continue. To lose heart is to say, "Even though I want to go on, I just can't go any farther."

Now, most of us have known what that feels like at some point. For many of us, it's become the way of life itself. Weariness is the new normal. Losing heart is a day-in and day-out reality. But the author of Hebrews wants us to know it doesn't have to be that way. He's given us example after example of those who stood up against the dangers and difficulties of their time and kept going despite the hardships.

They did it. They made it to the Hall of Heroes. They didn't throw in the towel. They risked. They set out. They believed. They stood up. They made choices based on what they truly believed in. As a result, they lived out the definition of faith. Their decisions became the substance of things hoped for and the evidence of things unseen. They made the seemingly unreachable, reachable after all. They made it because of where they chose to focus.

When I'm exercising on the treadmill, I simultaneously watch the news or other programming on TV. Focusing on the news enables me to endure the weariness of the treadmill. Similarly, focusing on Jesus provides the spiritual enablement to successfully endure the trials and stresses life brings our way. Where you focus your faith matters.

Keep in mind, faith is only as powerful as the object or being it's placed in. Put your faith in the tooth fairy, and you won't wind up with much of worth. On the contrary, God is real. He's the object of our hope. If God were not real, then faith would be like grasping after air.

For example, you'll often hear sports teams or athletes make statements like "I believe," with a period at the end of that sentence. Well, believe in what? That's not a complete understanding of faith, because

faith must include the substance. It must include the thing you're grabbing hold of. Belief in believing is never enough. Thus, the question of
faith always comes down to the worth of the object in which you place
your confidence.

Biblical faith isn't just a feeling. Neither is it an attitude or simply an
insignia on your T-shirt or hat. It's more than a saying you post on social
media. Biblical faith is grabbing hold of that which you cannot see in order
to access the authority and activity of the One in whom you placed your
faith. If your feet are still, and you are not moving, you don't have faith.
You may have emotions, but only actions reveal true faith.

A major difference exists between a high jumper and a pole vaulter. The
high jumper depends on his or her ability to jump over the bar. The pole
vaulter, however, depends on the pole to propel him or her much higher
than they could ever jump on their own. Biblical faith is grabbing hold of
Jesus Christ as the pole you lean on, which will enable you to go higher so
you can rise above the pain and problems that seek to defeat you.

The author of Hebrews wanted to remind any of us who feel discouraged that persevering brings about a reward. Walking by faith ushers in a
greater tomorrow. Even though things are tough, we're to maintain our
Christian commitment through the vicissitudes and challenges of life.

Pay Attention to Witnesses

Many of you may have grown up in the old church style, where as
he preached the preacher would often ask, "Can I get a witness?" Or he
might have said, "You have somebody who can testify!" In other words, he
was reminding his listeners they weren't the first people to be where they
were. Other people had gone through the fire and come out the other side
unscathed. What's more, they could testify about it.

Every year at year-end, we do employee evaluations for those who
work for our local and national ministries. This is the time when managers
seek to evaluate team members' work and their contribution to the overall mission. It's a time to show team members how much we value them

and their skills, to point out their strengths, and also to lovingly identify any weaknesses that can be improved upon.

We have a tremendous team that works for us at the national ministry, and, by and large, everyone hears a familiar phrase: "Well done." They experience an overall approval rating as we close out the year. Similarly, Hebrews 11 ends with this statement. We read in verse 39, "All these, having gained approval through their faith…"

These individuals the author of Hebrews mentions went through the difficulties and trials of life in such a way that they stood approved before God in the end. They heard the "well done" statement. And, what's more, they remain as legacies of faith to serve as inspiration to all of us. This is how they are referred to at the start of Hebrews 12 where it says, "Since we have so great a cloud of witnesses…" Or if you want to put that in the context of the Hall of Heroes setting, you could say, "Since we have so great a number of kingdom heroes…" The reminder is simple. Since they made it, you can too. Since they prevailed, you can prevail. Since they found a way, there's a way for you as well. What's more, they are available to support us as we run our Christian race.

Each of the heroes in these pages reminds us that, if all hope is gone, we can still go on. That's because we know the One greater than ourselves. They remind us that faith involves following God even when times are difficult.

It's easy to follow God when nothing is wrong. It becomes a greater challenge when everything is wrong. Yet God calls us to follow Him through the good times *and* the bad times. In doing so, we ultimately gain approval. We gain His evaluation that says, "Job well done." Or as the Bible says, "Well done, good and faithful slave" (Matthew 25:23).

Testimony after testimony after testimony reminds us of the truth of this eventual reward and approval. These are individuals who had chosen heaven over earth because they wanted something bigger. Their lives reflected a value system reflecting God's own, and they serve as an example to all of us. But it's up to you and me to pay attention to them. A testimony on its own won't make any difference in our lives. Only when we learn from it and apply the principles to our own choices will we benefit from what others have already learned and experienced.

See, I've noticed that one of the reasons people tend to give up is that they're surrounding themselves with the wrong kind of friends. They're hanging out with those who hold to a fatalistic, negative, secular worldview. That mindset can rub off on people. So one thing God wants us to keep in mind from our walk through this Hall of Heroes is that the company we keep impacts the internal climate of our soul. Why would we choose to hang out with someone heading the wrong direction spiritually? Other than to seek to disciple or mentor them, there's no good reason to do that. We are to hang out with those who will lift us and guide us into greater faith.

As I referenced in an earlier chapter, before a boxing match, former champions are often brought out to serve as inspiration to the boxers in the fight that day. By focusing on those who have gone before you, you find a deeper motivation for doing well yourself. You're not the only one who's been in this faith fight. You're not the only one who's had to wrestle with this spiritual conflict or be engaged in this battle.

Rather than face it alone and learn all your lessons from scratch, choose to surround yourself with the lives and lessons of those who have gone before you. Listen to those who have been where you are and still come out with a win. Sure, they may have been bruised a bit in the process, as all fighters have been, but when all was said and done, they raised their arm in victory. That's the great cloud of witnesses the writer of Hebrews is urging us to look toward for our own strength and motivation.

The cloud of witnesses reminds us that, as hard as life is, we are not to give up. As hard as the racial pandemic, medical pandemic, political pandemic, social pandemic, community pandemic, police pandemic, or your own personal pandemic might be—we are never to give up.

There exists a realm that is currently occupied by people who have gone on before us. My wife, my father, and my mother are in that realm. When Lois was preparing to transition to this eternal realm, she spoke of a reward.

She said they wanted to give her a reward, but they were just waiting for the song. Of course, that was a challenging thing to hear because we were all firmly placed in this realm. She, on the other hand, was very close to leaving this one for that other realm, so she was already engaging with it at some level.

There is a spiritual dimension we are to be partaking in as well. The Bible says in Ephesians 2:6 that God "raised us up with Him, and seated us with Him in the heavenly places in Christ Jesus." This spiritual realm includes an assembly who surrounds us because they are already there. They are in this spiritual dimension in heaven to which we are connected (Hebrews 12:22-24).

Thus, in some mysterious way, the people who have gone on before us in the faith are witnesses for our benefit today. While we're still on earth, they surround us in some way we cannot fully understand. But if we choose to live attached more to this spiritual location, even while we have a physical existence, we will gain insight, strength, and support from their testimonies and their joining in with the intercessory work of Jesus Christ on our behalf.

The problem is that we can become so tied up with the physical aspects of life that we don't know how to connect—or simply don't bother to connect—with the spiritual realm. Now, I can't say how all of this works because to my knowledge, the Bible doesn't go into all of that. But there is a network of support surrounding us who give testimony for our encouragement, strength, and correction. It's a heavenly presence that affords us spiritual benefits somehow. You can consider it like a Help Desk. When we are operating spiritually, by faith, based on the historical testimonies and spiritual interface with the Lord of those who have faithfully gone before us, we receive support and benefit from their wisdom and insight.

Not only that, but we are also to gain wisdom and insight from others who live faithfully on earth. This is one of the reasons God urges every Christian to be a part of a spiritual family. You might have heard me say this before, but I'm going to repeat it because it's that important. You don't need to go to church just to hear a sermon; you can hear a sermon online or on the radio. Neither do you need to go to church to worship; you can worship by yourself or listen to worship songs anytime through a variety of means. What church provides us is the opportunity to live in a community of believers. Church gives us a group of believers to hang out with, learn from, teach, and grow with. You are not created to proceed on this journey of faith alone. Just as we have a cloud of witnesses who provide unseen influence and support for us in the heavenly, spiritual realm, God has also provided visible witnesses for our support in the visible, earthly realm.

For example, if we were to flip a few pages back to Hebrews 10, we'd read this concept clearly.

> Let us hold fast the confession of our hope without wavering, for He who promised is faithful; and let us consider how to stimulate one another to love and good deeds, not forsaking our own assembling together, as is the habit of some, but encouraging one another; and all the more as you see the day drawing near (verses 23-25).

This Scripture says each of us ought to belong to a church as an assembly of believers to be involved in other people's lives. It gives us the opportunity to hang out with and inspire one another. That way, when someone's "get up and go" has "gotten up and gone," someone else will be there to encourage them forward.

One of the things we as a church wrestled with greatly, even before the mandatory lockdown here in the Dallas area, was how to spur a greater connectivity among our members. We didn't want church to be a place where people just showed up on Sunday to sit, soak, and then sour throughout the week because of a lack of ongoing engagement. Due to the busy nature of people's schedules—and later, the added difficulties ushered in with the multiple pandemics—Satan's strategy of keeping believers separate seemed to be working on a lot of levels. As we saw at the beginning of this chapter, depression and anxiety have soared in our nation over the last few years alone.

The design for all of us to help one another is community. We are to help one another "lay aside every encumbrance and the sin which so easily entangles us." We are to encourage one another to keep going and press on.

Shed Encumbrances and Unbelief

Keep in mind, an encumbrance isn't necessarily a bad thing in and of itself. It just holds you back from making your maximum progress because it's weighty. A racing runner or swimmer will wear the absolute minimum necessary because any additional weight is an encumbrance, holding them back from achieving their maximum speed and coming out victorious. In fact, swimmers have been known to shave their body hair to help them go as fast as they possibly can.

With regard to the spiritual life, encumbrances come in different shapes and sizes. But they're usually a noun—a place, a thing, or even a person.

Some of us can't fully run our kingdom race as a kingdom hero because people in our lives are stifling our movement. If we hang out with the wrong kind of people, we slow our own progress. Be wise in choosing your social circles. Places can also serve as encumbrances. Whether they divert our attention from God's principles or simply stir up our desire for greater pleasures, if they're holding us back they're an encumbrance.

The question on the floor isn't always whether a person or place is bad; the question is whether they're holding you back from maximizing your kingdom potential. Even things like television or hobbies can be an encumbrance if allowed to impede your forward movement as a disciple of Christ.

Now, again, I'm not saying these things are wrong in and of themselves. But if they're dominating your time and your mindset more than the Word of God or your relationship with Jesus is, then they're the kind of encumbrance the writer of Hebrews is talking about. And he says we're to do one thing and one thing only with those encumbrances: Lay them aside. Get rid of them. Set them down. Move on. Let go.

In addition to getting rid of encumbrances, the author of Hebrews also talks about getting rid of a specific sin. And while it's easy to identify obvious sins—failures to meet God's standards—the focus of these chapters in the book of Hebrews is the sin of unbelief. If you get rid of the sin of unbelief, you'll discover that you've dealt with a lot of your other sins as a result. The sin of unbelief sits at the root of nearly all sin. It's an entangling sin. It ties you up and keeps you bound in fear, doubt, worry, control, grief, and resentment. We also know this sin as the sin of faithlessness. It's such a far-reaching sin that it impacts everything else in your life.

It's like the college student who wanted to do his laundry without spending a lot of time on it, so he laid out a bedsheet and dumped his dirty clothes on it. Then he took the four corners of the sheet and tied them together, making a bundle before tossing it into the washer. But while he thought he was making his clothes clean, he was actually trapping the dirt and spreading it around. His clothes came out even dirtier because they'd been tangled together in one thing—the sheet.

Living with faithlessness will show up in every area of your life. It will show up in your emotions. It will show up in your words. It will show up in your actions. It will show up in your sleep cycles. It will show up in your health. It will show up in your finances. Faithlessness entangles all else, spreading the filth of unbelief to every intention, plan, and activity. Fundamentally, faithlessness is a failure to trust God, which is reflected by our refusal to act on what He has said, and a failure to trust God undermines everything He plans to do both in and through your life. It will literally abort His work in you.

Fix Your Eyes on Jesus

If you ever learn to believe God fully and demonstrate that by aligning your actions with His truth, you'll experience what it means to live as a kingdom hero yourself. You'll be able to "run with endurance the race that is set before" you, as the author of Hebrews encourages in Hebrews 12:1. You'll be able to keep pace with this long-distance run called the Christian life. And in Hebrews 12:2, you're told you'll be able to do that by "fixing [y]our eyes on Jesus, the author and perfecter of faith."

When you see *Jesus* in Scripture, the author is referring to His human name. *Christ* means Messiah. When you read about Jesus, you're reading about Him in His humanity. Thus, when Jesus lived on earth, He lived by faith. He was God, but He also functioned as a man. In His humanity, He modeled what it means to fully live by faith. As we're also told in Hebrews 12:2, He endured the difficulties of His life because of the "joy set before Him." He despised the shame because He knew where He would wind up: seated "at the right hand of the throne of God."

I guarantee if you fix your eyes on the troubles you're going through, you won't endure them. You have to fix your focus beyond the burdens. You have to follow Jesus' example of looking past the pain. Fixing your eyes on the difficulties would be similar to fixing your eyes on a donut while trying to stay on a weight-loss diet. That diet's not going to last very long. You need to look toward the goal in order to get past the grit and the grind in the grids of this life. One way to do this is to look to Jesus.

I believe the sun exists. I imagine you believe that too. But I don't believe the sun exists because I am looking at it. Rather, I believe it exists because I can see everything else due to its light. You and I may not physically see Jesus now, but when we focus on the resulting manifestations of who He is and what He has done, we are given the spiritual enablement and perspective to live life victoriously. We are given a new place to fix our gaze, rather than on the difficulties we face.

Jesus is both the author and the perfecter of your faith. To be the author means He's the originator. To be the perfecter means He's the completer. The author gets you started while the perfecter gets you finished. Jesus does both. In other words, He is your source for endurance and spiritual victory from beginning to end as you piggyback by faith on Him. He is the sum total of your faith; it is found in Him. As you abide in Him and His Word abides in you, you will access all you need to live a life of full and vibrant enduring faith.

Jesus was able to endure what He did on the cross because of the joy set before Him. What He saw and knew about His future resurrection, ascension, and exaltation motivated Him to keep going during the trials of daily life. In our contemporary culture, this is often comparable to students pursuing an advanced degree. The idea that graduation will soon be arriving helps them push through the studying, exams, and difficulties of obtaining that degree. Not all their classes may be their favorite, but if they choose to look at the goal of graduation rather than the monotony of enduring multiple math classes, for instance, they will push through. Similarly, if you can see something better off in the future, that will help you push through today.

One reason so many believers fail to live as kingdom heroes is that they begin to stare at what they're going through rather than look ahead to the joy set before them. So they stop walking *through* the trouble because they've become fixated *on* the trouble rather than on Jesus. Jesus is the author and finisher of your faith. He is the foundation upon which you are to stand. If you feel like life is too hard or you won't make it much longer, look to Him.

Listen for His voice. Set your gaze on His grace. Piggyback on His love, His confidence, and His assurance that He knows the plan for you. And it's a good plan. Your future is full of both good and hope. Jesus will give you the ability to keep going when you feel like all hope is gone. Not only that, but He'll give you the ability to rise higher and soar further than you ever thought possible. Never count yourself out of winding up in a hall like the one we've walked through in this book. Don't ever discount your contribution to the kingdom of God. You are a kingdom hero when you fully live out your purpose and destiny in Christ.

I never thought something I worked on—something I wrote—would wind up in a museum, not even after I passed away let alone while I was still alive! But that's exactly what happened with the Bible commentary I penned, presented both in one volume and in a study Bible. I didn't set out on the path of writing it because I thought it would be museum-worthy; I did that because I noticed a lack of easy-to-comprehend yet theologically sound commentary on Scripture available to everyday people. Sure, a number of heady commentaries for theologians pursuing advanced degrees exist, but last I checked, we're all to study the Word of God ourselves. So I wanted to create a tool for everyone. Not only that, but I saw nothing currently available that highlighted the threading of the all-important concept of the kingdom throughout the Bible.

So I set out on a decades-long journey of creating this voluminous work. Then just before these two items were released to the public, I got this word from the Museum of the Bible in Washington, DC. They were going to display the commentary and study Bible as an historic exhibit. I'll never forget finding that out during the celebration event for their release, held at our church.

During my late nights and countless early mornings of studying Scripture and detailing commentary, the thought or concept of an exhibit at that museum never crossed my mind. This was a wonderful surprise. But what kept me going through the tedious times was knowing that, when it was finished, this commentary would truly be one of a kind. It would be a first with an entirely kingdom focus. But it would also be a first by an African American in the history of our world. And it would be a first for anyone from the seminary I graduated from as well. And this view of the completion of the project pushed me through when things got busy and life itself got tough.

I want to encourage you to think beyond the moment you're in right now. You may not even be able to imagine what award or reward you could one day receive. I know I couldn't have as I worked on this commentary. But you can imagine that God knows what it is, and if it's from Him, it will be good.

I understand that life gets hard. Trust me, the last two years of the total ten-year focus of completing that large project were the toughest I'd ever had. But if you will press on and press through challenging times, keeping your eyes fixed on Jesus, who knows both the beginning and the end of your story, you'll experience everything you are to be and live out as a true kingdom hero.

Remember, a kingdom hero is a committed Christian who perseveres by faith in order to experience spiritual victory and divine approval. If you choose to persevere by faith, you just might wind up in the Hall of Heroes. You never know. You very well could be.

As we close our time together in this book, I want to share a story about a little girl who had been given a puzzle by her father. It was a 500-piece puzzle. As she began to work with all the various pieces, she began to cry in discouragement because she couldn't get things to fit. The protrusions and indentations wouldn't match up. She felt frustrated and wanted to quit.

Her father noticed her tears and asked her what was wrong. She told him she felt she couldn't do the puzzle. It just had too many pieces. But that's when the father took the top of the box and turned it over so she could see the picture. The puzzle he had brought her was a picture of Jesus. He said, "Dear, you've been trying to figure out how to put the pieces together one by one. But I want to change your approach. I want you to keep looking at the picture on the box. Keep looking at the picture of Jesus. Instead of trying to figure out each individual piece, focus on the picture. It will help you make sense of the whole puzzle."

Life comes with a lot of pieces, and sometimes trying to figure it all out and put it all together becomes too challenging. It can leave you crying. But I know one way we can all make it a lot simpler. If we will fix our eyes on Jesus, the author and finisher of our faith, we will get the big picture. When we focus on loving Him, living for Him, and serving Him, all the rest of the confusing pieces of life fall into place. That's what it means to live by faith. That's how a true kingdom hero maximizes his or her potential by pivoting his or her gaze from the problems to the Prince of all peace.

The bottom line, once again, is to never give up.

APPENDIX:
THE URBAN
ALTERNATIVE

The Urban Alternative (TUA) equips, empowers, and unites Christians to impact individuals, families, churches, and communities through a thoroughly kingdom-agenda worldview. In teaching truth, we seek to transform lives.

The core cause of the problems we face in our personal lives, homes, churches, and societies is a spiritual one. Therefore, the only way to address that core cause is spiritually. We've tried a political, social, economic, and even a religious agenda, and now it's time for a kingdom agenda.

The kingdom agenda can be defined as the visible manifestation of the comprehensive rule of God over every area of life.

The unifying central theme throughout the Bible is the glory of God and the advancement of His kingdom. The conjoining thread from Genesis to Revelation—from beginning to end—is focused on one thing: God's glory through advancing God's kingdom.

When we do not recognize that theme, the Bible becomes for us a series of disconnected stories that are great for inspiration but seem to be unrelated in purpose and direction. Understanding the role of the kingdom in Scripture increases our understanding of the relevancy of this several-thousand-year-old text to our day-to-day living. That's because God's kingdom was not only then; it is now.

The absence of the kingdom's influence in our personal lives, family lives, churches, and communities has led to a deterioration in our world of immense proportions:

- People live segmented, compartmentalized lives because they lack God's kingdom worldview.

- Families disintegrate because they exist for their own satisfaction rather than for the kingdom.

- Churches are limited in the scope of their impact because they fail to comprehend that the goal of the church is not its existence but its influencing the world for the kingdom.

- Communities have nowhere to turn to find real solutions for real people who have real problems because the church has become divided, ingrown, and unable to transform the cultural and political landscape in any relevant way.

By optimizing the solutions of heaven, the kingdom agenda offers us a way to see and live life with a solid hope. When God is no longer the final and authoritative standard under which all else falls, order and hope have left with Him. But the reverse is true as well: If God is still in the picture, and as long as His agenda is still on the table, we have hope. Even if relationships collapse, God will sustain us. Even if finances dwindle, God will keep us. Even if dreams die, God will revive us. As long as God and His rule are still the overarching standard in our lives, families, churches, and communities, hope remains.

Our world needs the King's agenda. Our churches need the King's agenda. Our families need the King's agenda.

We've put together a three-part plan to direct us to heal the divisions and strive for unity as we move toward the goal of truly being one nation under God. This three-part plan calls us to assemble with others in unity, to address the issues that divide us, and to act together for social impact. Following this plan, we will see individuals, families, churches, and communities transformed as we follow God's kingdom agenda in every area of our lives. You can request this plan by emailing info@tonyevans.org or by going online to tonyevans.org.

In many major cities, drivers can take a loop to the other side of the city when they don't want to head straight through downtown. This loop takes them close enough to the city center so they can see its towering buildings and skyline but not close enough to actually experience it.

This is precisely what we, as a culture, have done with God. We have put Him on the "loop" of our personal, family, church, and community lives. He's close enough to be at hand should we need Him in an emergency but far enough away that He can't be the center of who we are. We want God on the "loop," not the King of the Bible who comes downtown into the very heart of our ways. And as we have seen in our own lives and in the lives of others, leaving God on the "loop" brings about dire consequences.

But when we make God and His rule the centerpiece of all we think, do, or say, we experience Him in the way He longs for us to experience Him. He wants us to be kingdom people with kingdom minds set on fulfilling His kingdom's purposes. He wants us to pray, as Jesus did, "Not my will, but Thy will be done" because His is the kingdom, the power, and the glory.

There is only one God, and we are not Him. As King and Creator, God calls the shots. Only when we align ourselves under His comprehensive hand do we access His full power and authority in all spheres of life: personal, familial, ecclesiastical, and government.

As we learn how to govern ourselves under God, we then transform the institutions of family, church, and society using a biblically based kingdom worldview.

Under Him, we touch heaven and change earth.

To achieve our goal, we use a variety of strategies, approaches, and resources for reaching and equipping as many people as possible.

Broadcast Media

Millions of individuals experience *The Alternative with Dr. Tony Evans*, a daily broadcast on nearly 1,400 radio outlets and in over 130 countries. The broadcast can also be seen on several television networks and is available online at tonyevans.org. As well, you can listen to or view the daily broadcast by downloading the Tony Evans app for free in the App Store. Over 30,000,000 message downloads/streams occur each year.

Leadership Training

The *Tony Evans Training Center* (TETC) facilitates a comprehensive discipleship platform, which provides an educational program that embodies the ministry philosophy of Dr. Tony Evans as expressed through the kingdom agenda. The training courses focus on leadership development and discipleship in the following five tracks:

- Bible & Theology
- Personal Growth
- Family and Relationships
- Church Health and Leadership Development
- Society and Community Impact Strategies

The TETC program includes courses for both local and online students. Furthermore, TETC programming includes course work for non-student attendees. Pastors, Christian leaders, and Christian laity—both local and at a distance—can seek out the Kingdom Agenda Certificate for personal, spiritual, and professional development. For more information, visit tonyevanstraining.org.

Kingdom Agenda Pastors (KAP) provides a viable network for like-minded pastors who embrace the kingdom agenda philosophy. Pastors have the opportunity to go deeper with Dr. Tony Evans as they are given greater biblical knowledge, practical applications, and resources to impact individuals, families, churches, and communities. KAP welcomes senior and associate pastors of all churches. KAP also offers an annual

KAP Summit each year in Dallas with intensive seminars, workshops, and resources. For more information, visit: kafellowship.org

Pastors' Wives Ministry, founded by Dr. Lois Evans, provides counsel, encouragement, and spiritual resources for pastors' wives as they serve with their husbands in the ministry. A primary focus of the ministry is the KAP Summit, where senior pastors' wives are offered a safe place to reflect, renew, and relax, along with training in personal development, spiritual growth, and care for their emotional and physical well-being. For more information, visit loisevans.org.

Kingdom Community Impact

The outreach programs of The Urban Alternative seek to provide positive impact on individuals, churches, families, and communities through a variety of ministries. We see these efforts as necessary to our calling as a ministry and essential to the communities we serve. With training on how to initiate and maintain programs to adopt schools; provide homeless services; and partner toward unity and justice with the local police precincts, which creates a connection between the police and our community, we, as a ministry, live out God's kingdom agenda according to our *Kingdom Strategy for Community Transformation*.

The *Kingdom Strategy for Community Transformation* is a three-part plan that equips churches to have a positive impact on their communities for the kingdom of God. It also provides numerous practical suggestions for how this three-part plan can be implemented in your community, and it serves as a blueprint for unifying churches around the common goal of creating a better world for all of us. For more information, visit tonyevans.org, then click on the link to access the 3-Point Plan.

The *National Church Adopt-a-School Initiative* (NCAASI) prepares churches across the country to impact communities by using public schools as the primary vehicle for effecting positive social change in urban youth and families. Leaders of churches, school districts, faith-based organizations, and other nonprofit organizations are equipped with the knowledge and tools to forge partnerships and build strong social service delivery systems. This training is based on the comprehensive church-based community impact strategy conducted by Oak Cliff Bible Fellowship. It addresses such areas as economic development, education, housing, health revitalization, family renewal, and racial reconciliation. We assist churches in tailoring the model to meet specific needs of their communities while simultaneously addressing the spiritual and moral frame of reference. Training events are held annually in the Dallas area at Oak Cliff Bible Fellowship. For more information, visit churchadoptaschool.org.

Athlete's Impact (AI) exists as an outreach both into and through the sports arena. Coaches can be the most influential factor in young people's lives, even ahead of their parents. With the growing rise of fatherlessness in our culture, more young people are looking to their coaches for guidance, character development, meeting practical needs, and hope. Athletes fall just after coaches on the influencer scale. Whether professional or amateur, they influence younger athletes and kids within their spheres of impact. Knowing this, we aim to equip and train coaches and athletes on how to live out and utilize their God-given roles for the benefit of the kingdom. We aim to do this through our iCoach App as well as through resources such as *The Playbook: A Life Strategy Guide for Athletes*. For more information, visit icoachapp.org.

Tony Evans Films ushers in positive life change through compelling video-shorts, animation, and feature-length films. We seek to build kingdom disciples through the power of story; use a variety of platforms for viewer consumption and have over 100,000,000+ digital views; and merge video-shorts and film with relevant Bible study materials to bring people to the saving knowledge of Jesus Christ and to strengthen the body of Christ worldwide. Tony Evans Films released its first feature-length film, *Kingdom Men Rising*, in April 2019 in over 800 theaters nationwide and in partnership with Lifeway Films. The second release, *Journey with Jesus*, is in partnership with RightNow Media.

Resource Development

By providing a variety of published materials, we are fostering lifelong learning partnerships with the people we serve. Dr. Evans has authored more than 125 unique titles based on over 50 years of preaching—in booklet, book, or Bible-study format. He also holds the honor of writing the first full-Bible commentary by an African American. *The Tony Evans Study Bible* was released in 2019, and it sits in permanent display as a historic release in the Museum of the Bible in Washington, DC.

For more information and a complimentary copy of Dr. Evans's devotional newsletter, call (800) 800-3222; write to TUA at PO Box 4000, Dallas, TX, 75208; or visit us online at: www.tonyevans.org

ABOUT THE AUTHOR

Dr. Tony Evans is one of the country's most respected leaders in evangelical circles. He is a pastor, bestselling author, and frequent speaker at Bible conferences and seminars throughout the nation.

Dr. Evans has served as the senior pastor of Oak Cliff Bible Fellowship for more than 40 years, witnessing its growth from ten people in 1976 to more than 10,000 congregants with more than 100 ministries.

Dr. Evans also serves as president of The Urban Alternative, a national ministry that seeks to restore hope and transform lives through the proclamation and application of the Word of God. His daily radio broadcast, *The Alternative with Dr. Tony Evans*, can be heard on more than 1,400 radio outlets throughout the United States and in more than 130 countries.

Dr. Evans holds the honor of writing and publishing the first full-Bible commentary and study Bible by an African American. The study Bible and Commentary went on to sell more than 225,000 copies in its first year.

Dr. Evans is the former chaplain for the Dallas Cowboys and the Dallas Mavericks.

Through his local church and national ministry, Dr. Evans has set in motion a kingdom agenda philosophy of ministry that teaches God's comprehensive rule over every area of life as demonstrated through the individual, family, church, and society.

Dr. Evans was married to Lois, his wife and ministry partner of more than 50 years, until she transitioned to glory in late 2019. They are the proud parents of four, grandparents of 13, and great-grandparents of three.

Witness God's Power at Work in His People

Join Dr. Tony Evans on a six-week journey through the Bible's Hall of Faith: the heroes of the Old Testament whose acts of trusting God are spotlighted in Hebrews 11. As you study the stories of individuals like Abel, Noah, and Moses, you'll discover the life-altering confidence God asks you to have in Him—and how He can use that faith to transform you.

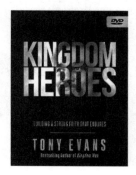

This recorded sermon series—which you can use in companion with Dr. Evans' *Kingdom Heroes Interactive Workbook*—will help you

- understand what it means to give God your very best
- remove any limits you may have placed on God's power
- live out your faith so that it grows stronger each day

Get ready to radically rely on God—and be amazed by how He changes your life!

Complete your experience with
Kingdom Heroes
Kingdom Heroes Interactive Workbook

"Faith is confidence in what we hope for and assurance about what we do not see."
—Hebrews 11:1

You must act out your faith before you can harvest the fruits of trusting God. But what does that look like in everyday life? As you look to people in the Bible who walked with assurance in God's power, you'll discover you can be confident that He will always provide for those who follow Him.

Dr. Tony Evans' *Kingdom Heroes Interactive Workbook*—which can be used on your own or with a group in companion with the *Kingdom Heroes DVD*—will help you refine your reliance on God's strength. Learn from the examples of biblical role models like Noah, Abraham, and Rahab so you can experience what it means to live by faith in your daily life.

Complete your experience with
Kingdom Heroes
Kingdom Heroes DVD

Building kingdom disciples.

At **The Urban Alternative,** our heart is to build kingdom disciples—a vision that starts with the individual and expands to the family, the church and the nation. The nearly 50-year teaching ministry of Tony Evans has allowed us to reach a world in need with:

The Alternative – Our flagship radio program brings hope and comfort to an audience of millions on over 1,400 radio outlets across the country.

tonyevans.org – Our library of teaching resources provides solid Bible teaching through the inspirational books and sermons of Tony Evans.

Tony Evans Training Center – Experience the adventure of God's Word with our online classroom, providing at-your-own-pace courses for your PC or mobile device. Visit tonyevanstraining.org.

Tony Evans app – This popular resource for finding inspiration on-the-go has had over 20,000,000 launches. It's packed with audio and video clips, devotionals, Scripture readings and dozens of other tools.

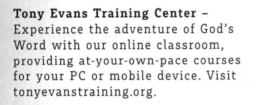

tonyevans.org

Life is busy,
but Bible study is still possible.

*a **portable** seminary*

Explore the kingdom.
Anytime, anywhere.

Subscription model

TONY EVANS
TRAINING CENTER

tonyevanstraining.org

MORE GREAT
HARVEST HOUSE BOOKS BY
DR. TONY EVANS

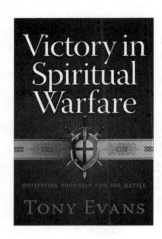

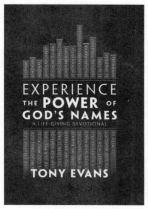

EXPERIENCE THE POWER OF GOD'S NAMES
A LIFE-GIVING DEVOTIONAL
TONY EVANS

EXPERIENCING GOD TOGETHER
How Your Connection with Others Deepens Your Relationship with God
TONY EVANS

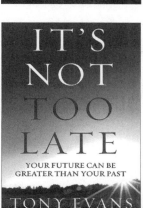

IT'S NOT TOO LATE
YOUR FUTURE CAN BE GREATER THAN YOUR PAST
TONY EVANS
BESTSELLING AUTHOR

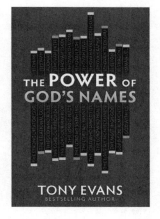

THE POWER OF GOD'S NAMES
TONY EVANS
BESTSELLING AUTHOR

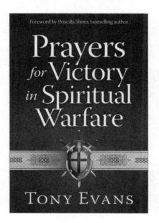

Foreword by Priscilla Shirer, bestselling author
Prayers for Victory in Spiritual Warfare
TONY EVANS

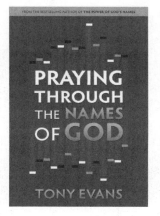

FROM THE BESTSELLING AUTHOR OF THE POWER OF GOD'S NAMES
PRAYING THROUGH THE NAMES OF GOD
TONY EVANS